Testing Too Much?

Testing Too Much?

A Principal's Guide to Cutting Back Testing and Reclaiming Instructional Time

Philip A. Streifer

with contributions by Barry Sheckley and Richard Ayers

ROWMAN & LITTLEFIELD
Lanham • Boulder • New York • London

Published by Rowman & Littlefield
A wholly owned subsidary of The Rowman & Littlefield Publishing Group, Inc.
4501 Forbes Boulevard, Suite 200, Lanham, Maryland 20706
www.rowman.com

Unit A, Whitacre Mews, 26-34 Stannary Street, London SE11 4AB

British Library Cataloguing in Publication Information Available

Library of Congress Cataloging-in-Publication Data Available

ISBN: 978-1-4758-3366-9 (cloth : alk. paper)
ISBN: 978-1-4758-3367-7 (pbk : alk. paper)
ISBN: 978-1-4758-3368-3 (electronic)

∞ ™ The paper used in this publication meets the minimum requirements of American National Standard for Information Sciences Permanence of Paper for Printed Library Materials, ANSI/NISO Z39.48-1992.

Printed in the United States of America

Contents

Acknowledgments

This subject matter and my views on the related topics evolved over time, as I note in the epilogue. My two friends and colleagues Barry Sheckley and Dick Ayers helped frame these views over many years. I'm appreciative that they agreed to contribute chapters that greatly enhanced the themes proposed in the book. Through Facebook posts on this topic, I reconnected with a high school friend who spent his career teaching history and government on Long Island, NY. Thomas Cook's experiences turned out to fit beautifully with the main theme, and thus I'm extremely grateful for his willing participation in sharing his work. Finally, to my wife, thanks for coaxing me to finish this challenging book when too often I preferred to find other things to do.

Introduction

The evidence is clear—children are tested too much these days. But not all testing is bad; in fact, you could make an independent case to keep just about all the testing that already goes on in your school today. So how do you decide what to keep and what to drop if there is just too much of it taking up students' days? And in the higher grades, where departmentalization is so prevalent, how do you cut back on testing when the challenge is as much a political school endeavor as an academic one?

The argument in this book is straightforward: (1) Children, especially in urban settings, need more time to learn, but schools do not have sufficient funds to pay for this added time; and (2) schools are testing too much, and they need to cut back responsibly on testing, with a plan, and use that saved time for instruction. Schools should not, however, abandon all testing, as some would argue. Doing so would return American public education to the era of the 1980s and 1990s, when testing and data were not the driving decision-making forces in public education they are today—and when there was little accountability. That laissez-faire attitude left a policy vacuum, resulting in a politically driven overreliance on tests that created a pressure-cooker school environment, which is unhealthy for both kids and teachers. Thus, the purpose of this book is to find a balance, to set forth a logical plan that principals and data teams responsibly can use to reduce the total amount of testing that students experience, and to propose a way to best use that recaptured instructional time.

IS IT A TEST OR AN ASSESSMENT?

A definition of terms is important, so to start we should ask whether there is a difference between *test* and *assessment*. An *educational test* is defined by Merriam-Webster as a " test that measures achievement in subjects of study." An *assessment* is defined as the "act of making a judgment about something." However, the terms are often used interchangeably by educators to describe an activity that determines what students know.

For the purposes of this book—that is, the focus on if we are testing too much—it is not useful to make a distinction between tests and assessments because we are focusing on the amount of time these activities take in a school year. Regardless of whether activities students engage in are formally defined as tests or assessments, if they take up class time, we lump them into the same category. To stay with common nomenclature, when discussing *assessment* audits, we use that term. However, they could just as easily be called *testing* audits because they typically catalogue all the sit-down, paper-and-pencil or computer tests kids take.

The main point is this: In determining whether instructional time can be recaptured, we use the terms *test* and *assessment* interchangeably to describe all forms of sit-down activities that are paper-and-pencil responses (but could be computer-adaptive, too), where students are tested on what they know. If we were discussing teacher observation and judgment of student performance as a replacement for some of these sit-down tests, then it would be a clearer distinction, and using the term *assessment* in that regard would be much more appropriate. Later chapters discuss this issue, but for the purposes of recapturing instructional time, we define every activity where districts, schools, and teachers require students to sit and respond as a test.

HOW DID WE GET HERE?

Essentially educators dropped the ball on accountability during the 1980s and 1990s. Public education did not respond well to the "Nation at Risk" report, which argued, somewhat illegitimately, based on the actual evidence, that American public schools were failing.[1] Not all schools were failing, but some kids were not performing well for a host of socioeconomic and racial-segregation reasons. Our collective failure to respond in a concerted manner led to further attempts to shake up the system.

Bill Clinton's Goals 2000 program, led largely by U.S. corporate CEOs and governors, also failed to move the goalposts. The "Nation at Risk Report" came out in 1983; the Goals 2000 initiative started with the Clinton administration in the early 1990s[2] but failed to achieve its stated goals by the time of the 2000 national election. That brought us to 2001 and the unique political partnership between President Bush and Senator Ted Kennedy, along with near-unanimous approval by Congress of the No Child Left Behind Act, which, for the first time, leveraged federal Title I funding based on student success on state-administered standardized tests. By focusing on money, the national government finally caught our attention!

Since then, public education collectively overreacted, testing just about everything that could be tested and evaluating things that should never be measured with standardized tests. And when not enough progress was being made each year on adequate yearly progress (AYP), federal and state governments institutionalized teacher evaluation based on standardized testing of students, even though most poorly performing schools were grossly underfunded and undersupplied.

As teachers became frustrated and began speaking out, a parent-led "dropout movement" emerged that now argues for the elimination of all, or most, standardized tests. The federal government, in response, suggested recently that no more than 3 percent of a student's school year be devoted to testing. But in reality, most kids experience 10 percent or more of their year in testing and testing-related activities (more on this later for those questioning the numbers).

Instructional time is the most important resource schools have. Think about it: Every other resource or input a school has is designed to support or promote instructional time. And it is a fixed resource. There is just so much of it, and once it's used up, it's gone.

The federal government's suggestion that students only spend about 3 percent of their school year in testing amounts to 5½ days (in a typical 180-day school year). But this refers to testing for federal and state accountability, which is not going away anytime soon! If one counts all the other tests kids take, teacher-made and vendor-provided, it can easily amount to 10 percent or more, depending on grade level. That's a whopping eighteen days!

If educators could cut that by 25 percent, each student would gain four and a half instructional days a year! Cut that by 50 percent, and it amounts to nine days saved per year. Teachers could use that time for instruction, and poorer-performing and underachieving students desperately need that extra time for learning. Consider for a moment what adding five to ten instructional days per year would mean in each student's school life—and at no additional cost to the school district, city or town, or state! Achieving these savings would be a win-win for all involved. But what should teachers do with that newly found instructional time?

Barry Sheckley has found that learning improves dramatically when teachers enhance student self-regulation in the learning process. But teaching teachers to "let go" is not so easy, and teacher-directed instruction is not helping students to learn to set their own personal learning goals. Sheckley finds that when these shifts in instructional approach are achieved, the results are impressive. A goal of this book is to explain how this shift can occur, what the steps involved are, and how to use recaptured time from unnecessary or duplicative nonmandated student testing to improve learning.

Principals and data teams are in a bind, though—caught between political pressure to provide evidence of student success and having to respond to the needs of teachers, parents, and kids who want less testing. They know that difficult decisions about students, their placements, class grades, class rank, and graduation rely on "having the facts" regardless of what the opt-out folks say. And even if they tackled the issue directly, on what basis would they advocate for keeping or dropping various tests?

This book provides a rationale for making these decisions together with teachers, district-level administrators, and parents using a two-part framework. First and foremost, we focus on which tests teachers *actually use* and gain the most value from in assessing student learning in a way that guides ongoing instruction. Second, of these, educators should select tests that are most valuable from a test soundness point of view. Here we tackle in basic terms the issues of test reliability and validity but in ways that are easily understood by all audiences.

To address the first issue, which tests are used, the book provides a framework of the various types of tests, what each is used for, and what information each type should *not* be relied on to provide. To address the soundness issue and to strike a good balance of types of tests and assessments to use, our framework allows users to rate each on the degree to which it likely measures what it was intended to measure and whether it does so with regularity. Our proposal carves out a special place for so-called authentic assessment because, properly done, these assessments both teach and are useful in determining what students know. The challenge here is how to do them correctly and in a meaningful way to achieve these dual goals.

We also want to take time to talk about the value of daily teacher observation and judgment for the task of assessing student learning. Our experience tells us that teachers are rarely wrong when basing decisions about readiness and learning from their daily work and interaction with students. But they have been pressured into "showing the facts," as it were, that students are doing well or not. Our framework will help teachers balance the tests they eliminate with their own judgments so a more sensible method is used and relied on to satisfy all audiences.

What should be the guiding principle of schooling? As we've seen since 2001, the shift has been toward more measurement, often at the expense of sound instruction, the arts, social studies, and the sciences in the early grades. Evaluating teachers through standardized tests has had a detrimental impact on school culture. In chapter 8, Dick Ayers lays out a more humanistic approach to schooling rooted in a focus on child development, not the politics of a "box-score" mentality that has so driven American public school thinking over the past couple decades.

As a guidebook, we seek to achieve two super goals. First, we want to explain these issues in sufficient detail but not in an overly technical way to help principals define their thinking such that they can "make the case" to their various constituencies. Second, we strive to provide a framework on which to decide which tests to keep, which to discard, the reasons for doing so, and how to develop a more balanced approach to assessing student learning in a way that recaptures precious instructional time. Once that time is recaptured, Barry Sheckley suggests that teachers can be far more effective if they help students take more control over their learning, setting their own personal learning goals and even strategies.

As authors and practitioners, we have lived in the world of data-driven decision making for a very long time. Most of the positions and arguments this book makes is from my lifetime of professional experiences. For most of those years, schools, including mine, operated based on the belief that tests and measurement would be the answer to improve schooling.

However, the field has now learned that teachers largely do not understand what the test results mean or how to use them. They often misinterpret and use the statistics and reports incorrectly. The reports themselves are often so complicated that, even with summer training, teachers just do not know or remember what all the numbers mean when the reports come back in the late fall or early winter. As busy people, they did not have the time to relearn it all. The result: Too many times we find teachers privately admitting that they just do not use the results.

REVIEW OF CHAPTERS

Chapter 1, "Accountability on Steroids: How We Got Here," describes in some detail the growth of the accountability movement that permeates every aspect of public educational life today. The outgrowth of this singular focus on accountability by high-level policy makers has been an overreliance on standardized testing that inevitably led to many parents objecting to testing and today's growing parental opt-out movement, where parents keep their kids home from school on testing days.

Chapter 2 takes a different tack on this issue, suggesting that the law is the law until changed and that parents should not opt out and educators should do all that they can to make the most use of these tests (which is typically not the case). By doing so, they can help parents understand various tests' value by displaying and discussing the results in detail and what is done with those results. Thus, the title of this chapter is "It's the Law: Helping Parents Choose to Not Opt Out."

Just how much are we testing? Chapter 3 describes the school day and year from a student's point of view at the elementary, middle, and high school levels. It identifies all or most of the testing that occurs and separates out all the nonmandated, unnecessary, or duplicative testing that is likely used in public schools. The key idea is to focus on nonmandated testing for making reductions, while making much better and full use of testing that is still required.

But how does one decide what to keep and what to discard? This is where validity and reliability come into play, and chapter 4 tackles (or constructs) these complex ideas in a way that we hope can be readily understood and applied without needing a doctorate in testing and evaluation! This chapter also includes a list of typically asked questions and responses written in everyday language.

Having laid down this foundation of usability, chapter 5 gets to the core of the book by providing three models for use in reducing the amount of nonmandated testing. Each model is viable in its own right, but the degree of complexity grows from methods 1 to 2 to 3, depending on the level of knowledge the reader has with the science of test and measurement. Folks not well steeped in the science of measurement will want to look at the first model, whereas those with strong testing backgrounds should look at the third model.

A book on reducing testing to recapture instructional time would be incomplete without discussing the importance of instructional time itself, thus chapter 6 presents a review of literature on the topic. This chapter is intended to provide the theoretical foundation on which the core argument of the book is predicated. Anyone disputing the value of instructional time, especially for underprivileged students, should carefully review what the research says. This chapter also reviews what it typically costs to increase time in traditional ways, such as adding to the length of the school day and year, concluding that it is just too expensive to do so and thus an alternative strategy is needed.

What would a rethinking of instruction look like in this new approach? Chapter 7 provides an example at the high school level, where the most amount of instructional time can likely be reclaimed. But these same strategies apply at the elementary and middle school levels, as well. So, this chapter provides an example from practice on how instruction and assessment can change. High school was chosen for this in-depth example because, of the three levels, high schools are the least changed and in dire need of redesign.

Chapter 8 focuses on school culture and what boards of education, superintendents, and principals need to do to create a working environment safe enough for teachers to experiment with these changes. Culture is one of the most important aspects of effective organizations, and one could say that, as the culture is defined, so goes the organization. After almost twenty years of top-down, test-driven accountability, school organizations have responded accordingly. No school reform effort is going to be successful without somehow addressing the cultural conditions that will encourage teachers and principals to make meaningful changes.

In chapter 9, Barry Sheckley details his work with teachers on how they can transform instruction and assessment at the elementary and middle school levels. Barry demonstrates how learning improves when teachers stop teaching (direct instruction) and instead focus on promoting student engagement in their own learning. Barry's life work is on how self-regulation is a key component of deeper learning.

Finally, chapter 10 provides a retrospective of my experiences over the years as a data-driven, testing-focused superintendent of schools. Hindsight being twenty-twenty, that strategy did not work out very well in the overall scheme of things, leading to a realization and rationale as to why change is needed.

Having a testing and measurement background, my disappointment (and disillusionment) grew at the degree to which most educators just do not know how to use testing results. No one would responsibly argue that schools forsake all testing. But a good case can now be made that schools should embrace a more responsible testing policy seeking a reduction of nonmandated testing by a small amount (25 percent) to achieve a better balance among the needs of our students.

My last assignment was in a fringe urban district, in contrast to my earlier positions in high-performing suburban districts. The impact of poverty on student learning was very real here. These kids need more instructional time to make up for the lifetime deficits they come to kindergarten with, only to fall further and further behind through elementary school.

It was easy to become frustrated with the lack of adequate financial support and the futility of trying to add a few minutes onto a school day or maybe add a day onto the school year. The result was a need of an alternative strategy for the clear majority of public noncharter schools to find that much-needed extra time.

This book is for superintendents, curriculum directors, teachers, and principals who desire a way to cut back on student testing in a thoughtful and defensible manner. Unlike the "opt-out movement," our approach is not to end all testing but to use tests sparingly and to rely more on teacher judgment, buoyed by those tests that are retained. And we want to help teachers improve student learning in a way that we know works by encouraging students to take more responsibility in their own active learning.

Having been there, we understand and are in awe of what teachers and principals need to do to be successful today. We hope that our guidebook proves useful in their mission.

NOTES

1. Berliner, David C., and Bruce Jesse Biddle. *The manufactured crisis: Myths, fraud, and the attack on America's public schools*. Reading, MA: Addison-Wesley, 1995.

2. Goals 2000: Educate America Act, Pub. L. No. 103-227 (1994). http://uscode.house.gov/statutes/pl/103/227.pdf.

Chapter One

Accountability on Steroids

How We Got Here

Let's face it: Schools are testing kids much too much today. They test and try to evaluate just about everything in sight, driven by an accountability movement that has its roots in the 1950s and has grown in intensity ever since. The good news is that there appears to be some breathing room with the recent passage of the Every Student Succeeds Act (ESSA) of 2015. Not all testing is bad; in fact, one could make an independent argument in favor of just about all the testing that typically goes on in schools. The problem is that there is just too much of it. Although schools cannot cut back on state- or federally mandated tests, there are still a lot of other tests that could be scaled back or outright eliminated.

It was not always this way—this intense accountability that is so much part of school life today. In fact, prior to 2001, when the No Child Left Behind Act (NCLB) was signed into law, life in schools was very different. Teachers and principals who started their careers post-2001 are living in such a different world that going back to 1990s would seem like a time warp. So, how did we get here—to the latter part of the second decade of the twenty-first century, where everything is tested and measured?

Understanding the history that led up to what some see as necessary accountability and others (like the opt-out movement) view as over-testing that is ruining public schooling can help one develop a position on these issues. At the very least, it helps explain how we got to this point.

Most chapters like this one start with something akin to "The report 'A Nation at Risk' began a new era in American public education." But, in fact, we can trace the roots of discontent with the public schools back much further. "A Nation at Risk" was published in 1983, but the nation was becoming frustrated and losing confidence in its public institutions and government much earlier.

The United States emerged from the Second World War a powerhouse in terms of international influence and military power. The 1950s also brought forth great levels of American prosperity as President Eisenhower successfully kept the country out of war[1] despite the desires of many of the nation's generals at the time. The country was on a roll; people were employed, and the standard of living was improving, with many buying homes and automobiles. The real standard of living for most Americans was never higher. But there was a looming threat—the Soviet Union.

Sputnik shocked America. It was October 4, 1957. All of a sudden, the United States no longer reigned supreme, and with the Soviet Union now possessing nuclear weapons, the threat seemed all the more ominous. School-kids practiced "duck and cover" drills to shield themselves from flying glass after a nuclear explosion. The nation was nervous, and that led to a space race.

President Kennedy announced before Congress on May 25, 1961, the goal of sending an American to the moon before the end of the decade. His reason was to catch up to and hopefully overtake the Russians in space and missile technology. While the United States succeeded with the moon landing in 1969, tensions with the Soviet Union did not abate, resulting in several proxy wars around the globe.

Kennedy also tried but failed to oust the Cuban Communist government in the Bay of Pigs invasion. That led to near world catastrophe with the Cuban Missile Crisis of 1962, which came perilously close to ending with a nuclear exchange between the superpowers. The overwhelming American superiority of world power that we enjoyed during the early to mid-1950s now seemed like a long-lost memory.

Then, like a bolt, Kennedy was assassinated in November 1963. All historical indications were that he was going to withdraw from Southeast Asia and even wanted to join with the Russians in a joint moon landing project to help bridge the two nations' differences. Instead, Johnson became president, and during the following decade, from the mid-1960s to the mid-1970s,

Vietnam shook Americans' confidence in their government. The Vietnam War ended with the fall of Saigon on April 30, 1975.

During this time, America endured the Nixon era of prolonged war in Southeast Asia and scandal. There were street protests across the country and then Watergate in 1972, which led to (largely due to his cover-up) Nixon's resignation from office in disgrace in the middle of his second term in 1974.

Some say that it was the Nixon administration that heralded mistrust in government and its institutions among the populace. A better way to look at it is as a tipping point from all these events since World War II. Either way, America's unbridled confidence and trust in its political institutions just has not been the same since. And public schools are part of that set of institutions.

Jimmy Carter's administration saw the Iranian revolution and the capture of America's diplomats. There was a failed military operation to rescue the hostages. (They were finally released upon Reagan's swearing in in January 1981.) The nation saw inflation and interest rates soar during this period, with the so-called misery index (unemployment plus inflation) hitting new heights, which Reagan successfully used to his advantage during the campaign, famously asking whether Americans were better off today than when Carter assumed the presidency. For those of us who lived during that era, we will remember 15 to 18 percent home mortgage rates as the norm!

Ronald Reagan was elected president, and it was in 1983, during his early administration, that "A Nation at Risk" was published. Here we see in some ways, for the first time, a focus on the nation's schools. True, Sputnik spawned an interest and focus on science education, but "A Nation at Risk" was a damming indictment of the American public school system, and it called for structural change. Bill Bennett was Reagan's secretary of education from 1985 to 1988, and he pushed an aggressive agenda that American schools needed serious reform.

Bill Clinton (president from 1993 to 2001) took this school improvement effort in a different direction, pushing his Goals 2000 agenda, which was enacted into law in 1994. Goals 2000 established a framework to develop world-class goals for America's schools. This bill was intended to

> improve learning and teaching by providing a national framework for education reform; to promote the research, consensus building, and systemic changes needed to ensure equitable educational opportunities and high levels of educational achievement for all American students; . . . [and] to promote the

development and adoption of a voluntary national system of skill standards and certifications.[2]

Driven in large part by the corporate community, the goals were wide-reaching and stated:

By the Year 2000 . . .

- All children in America will start school ready to learn.
- The high school graduation rate will increase to at least 90 percent.
- All students will leave grades 4, 8, and 12 having demonstrated competency over challenging subject matter including English, mathematics, science, foreign languages, civics and government, economics, the arts, history, and geography, and every school in America will ensure that all students learn to use their minds well, so they may be prepared for responsible citizenship, further learning, and productive employment in our nation's modern economy.
- United States students will be first in the world in mathematics and science achievement.
- Every adult American will be literate and will possess the knowledge and skills necessary to compete in a global economy and exercise the rights and responsibilities of citizenship.
- Every school in the United States will be free of drugs, violence, and the unauthorized presence of firearms and alcohol and will offer a disciplined environment conducive to learning.
- The nation's teaching force will have access to programs for the continued improvement of their professional skills and the opportunity to acquire the knowledge and skills needed to instruct and prepare all American students for the next century.
- Every school will promote partnerships that will increase parental involvement and participation in promoting the social, emotional, and academic growth of children.[3]

Unfortunately, it did not work, as history has shown. Many see the No Child Left Behind Act of 2001 as the next logical step to drive improvement.

Not everyone was buying the premise that America's schools were failing. In 1996, David Berliner and Bruce Biddle published a fairly popular book titled *The Manufactured Crisis: Myths, Fraud, and the Attack on America's Public Schools* that uncovered many of the falsehoods being promulgated as truths in "A Nation at Risk."[4] Although it makes a very convincing case that much of the hype of poor and failing schools was just that, it nevertheless failed to have the widespread political impact the authors hoped for.

Phil Streifer was superintendent of schools in Avon, Connecticut, at the time. He recalls hearing, together with fellow Connecticut superintendents, an address by their senator at the time, Chris Dodd. Dodd implored them to take hold of the educational agenda, to own accountability in an effort to improve schools, or Congress, he warned, would do it for us. Well, collectively school leaders at all levels failed, which led to the No Child Left Behind Act of 2001.

For the first time, the national government was not playing around with goals and improvement frameworks. So much for input measures and process goals! The government mandated outcome measures as the focal point of school improvement in the form of student testing in math and reading for all students in grades 3 to 8, mandated that states set up strict accountability standards known as adequate yearly progress, and held Title I funding hostage if states failed to comply. The feds focused on money and caught educators' attention.

At just around the same time, America experienced the worst attack on the homeland since Pearl Harbor with the 9/11 terrorist attacks in New York, Pennsylvania, and Washington, DC. The national focus was now on terrorism and war in Afghanistan and Iraq and against al-Qaeda—not on public education. While President George W. Bush was a strong supporter of NCLB, having won almost unanimous bipartisan support in Congress (including that of Senator Ted Kennedy), his focus was now on national security and war. And the promised added resources for education never materialized, even though they were a well-known condition of Democratic support for the bill.

To most educators during that time, NCLB was hard to argue against. Many perceived the lack of educational progress as real and bought fully into the national agenda. SAT scores were flat; international test score comparisons showed the United States consistently behind other countries, such as on PISA (Program for International Student Assessment); and the nation was at war with al-Qaeda and Iraq—so it was not a time to balk.

Barack Obama was elected president in 2008 on a platform to bring the troops home responsibly and focus on the economy. The economy had just crashed during the election campaign, which brought about the Great Recession of 2008, although to many Americans it might as well have been the second Great Depression, with massive losses of jobs, homes, and savings.

The dramatic fall of Wall Street had many jokingly referring to their 403(b) retirement savings as 203(b)s or, at its bottom, 103(b)s! It was not funny, though; it was tough times.

President Obama and Arne Duncan, his education secretary, doubled down on NCLB, with new rules requiring that student testing results be used in teacher evaluation. Obama also won from Congress billions for massive experimentation in educational innovation called "Race to the Top." However, history has not judged these interventions well. None of this appears to have worked, with the achievement gap improving only marginally since the 1990s or in 2001.

Diane Ravitch commented recently in her blog (just prior to ESSA passage),

> Despite the lack of evidence for tying teacher evaluation to student test scores, despite the hundreds of millions spent to implement it without success, this is Arne Duncan's line in the sand. He insists on mandated annual testing, because without it, his idea of teacher evaluation crashes. He doesn't care that most teachers don't teach tested subjects. It is not the annual tests he loves, it is the teacher grades based in annual test scores. [5]

NCLB was recently reauthorized by Congress by passing the Every Child Succeeds Act (ESSA), which was signed into law in December 2015. In the final analysis, ESSA does loosen the reins a bit, freeing up states and local school districts from some of the onerous testing demands of NCLB. And now there will be no role for the federal government mandating testing for teacher evaluation. Duncan left office, and Obama transitioned to private life following the inauguration of Donald Trump.

As of November 2016, there was little discussion of education policy from either national party, its presidential candidates, or President Trump. That is likely due to the fact that Trump will have little influence over educational policy given the recent passage of ESSA 2015.

But the damage is done. There is now a vibrant, national, testing opt-out movement. In 2015, more than a half-million students did not take their NCLB tests, and one in five New York students opted out. [6] Parents are reacting to stressed-out teachers and their children with simple acts of defiance, and it remains to be seen what happens this year after passage of ESSA.

As 2017 is beginning, testing and test-based accountability have a bad name, and the knee-jerk reaction of many is to just throw out the tests altogether. Congress basically did so in ESSA, leaving it largely up to the states as to how to proceed. It is highly unlikely, though, that much will change.

But not all testing is bad. The problem is that there is just too much of it, and these tests have been used in ways they were never intended for, such as evaluating schools and teachers. School principals and teachers need to strike a more reasonable balance between and among the various forms of testing students experience daily, weekly, monthly, and yearly.

SUMMARY

Given history, it's easy to understand how we wound up with NCLB in 2001. And given world events at that time and since, it's also easy to understand how NCLB, along with its testing for school evaluation and teacher evaluation, became so entrenched in our national psyche in the years between 2001 and 2016.

But the pressures on teachers and schools to perform against unreasonable odds (and little-understood national standards) also helps to better understand why so many parents are just saying "no" now. While Congress listened and did loosen some testing requirements in ESSA 2015, accountability is here to stay. The time has now come to strike a better balance, to use standardized and other tests for the purposes for which they were designed, and to create school and teacher accountability programs that make sense and are fundamentally fair.

Recently, the federal government called for no more than 3 percent of a student's school year to be spent in testing. But they meant standardized testing for accountability. Three percent amounts to about 5½ days based on a 180-day school year. Kids experience a whole lot more testing and evaluation in schools, and in the higher the grades, with departmentalization, the number of hours and days spent in testing versus learning only goes up. It can easily amount to 10 percent or more (much more in some cases).

If we could cut the amount of testing back by 25 percent, that would restore a lot of instructional time. And, if teachers would rely more on their own judgment and authentic assessments in which assessment and learning are the same activity, then even more time is gained. The remainder of this book is focused on helping teachers and principals achieve this goal.

NOTES

1. Thomas, Evan. *Ike's bluff: President Eisenhower's secret battle to save the world*. New York: Little, Brown, 2012.

2. King, Erika F. "Goals 2000: Educate America Act." *School Law Bulletin* 25, no. 4 (1994): 15–27.

3. Goals 2000: Educate America Act, Pub. L. No. 103-227 (1994). http://us-code.house.gov/statutes/pl/103/227.pdf.

4. Berliner, David C., and Bruce Jesse Biddle. *The manufactured crisis: Myths, fraud, and the attack on America's public schools*. Reading, MA: Addison-Wesley, 1995.

5. Ravitch, Diane. "What is the future of test-based teacher evaluation?" *Diane Ravitch's Blog*. January 29, 2015. https://dianeravitch.net/2015/01/29/what-is-the-future-of-test-based-teacher-evaluation.

6. Schweig, Jonathan. "The opt-out reckoning." *U.S. News & World Report*. May 9, 2016. http://www.usnews.com/opinion/articles/2016-05-09/who-does-the-movement-to-opt-out-of-standardized-testing-help.

Chapter Two

It's the Law

Helping Parents Choose to Not Opt Out

There is an active populist political movement alive and well in this country as evidenced by the 2016 presidential race and election of Donald J. Trump. Not limited to the United States, the recent Brexit vote in the United Kingdom is another example, as are the many antitrade and anti-immigration movements bubbling up in Western countries.

The antitesting, or opt-out, movement similarly is a populist reaction to nationally mandated (Common Core) standards and standardized testing here in the United States. Brought on by too much testing in general and using NCLB/ESSA tests for purposes for which they were not designed, parental reactions to having their kids sit through these tests year after year are understandable. But just because opting out may be the populist thing to do, it does not make it right. As principals and teachers, it should be your role to help parents understand the proper use of these tests and why they should not have their kids opt out.

Unfortunately, the new Every Student Succeeds Act that took effect in 2016 is not helping much. Although there is some confusion on this issue, as of this writing, it appears to require that states continue enforcing the 95 percent rule (that 95 percent of students take the tests in each district), but it also says that states can allow parents to opt out, according to responses Diane Ravitch received from Senator Alexander's office in January 2016.[1] (Lamar Alexander was one of the primary architects of the law.)

Ravitch asked, "What does the law say about parent opt outs from testing? Are states allowed to withhold funding from schools where the participation rate is less than 95%?" The response is important:

- Under ESSA, in section 1111(b)(2)(K) of the new law, states are allowed, if they choose, to allow parents to opt students out of the federally required 17 tests.
- In section 1111(c)(4)(E) of the new law, states are required to ensure that 95 percent of all students participate in the federally required 17 tests.
- But, in that same section, the federal requirement is that, as part of the state accountability system, states determine how to take into account—or "factor"—the participation rate of students in determining how to judge the schools within the state. The Secretary, in section 1111(e)(1)(B)(iii)(XI) of the new law, is prohibited from telling a state how that requirement must be factored into the state accountability system. This means that the Secretary cannot say a school must drop a rating in the state accountability system, or be forced to enter into some kind of school improvement, or dictate any solution from Washington. How the 95 percent requirement factors into the state accountability system and the consequences for a school that fails to meet the 95 percent requirement are state decisions.
- As under NCLB, the new law allows the Secretary to withhold Title I administrative funds if a state does not measure 95 percent of all students (or meet other requirements of the law).
- However, it is up to the state, and not the Secretary, to enforce the 95 percent requirement for schools and determine the consequences for schools who do not meet the 95 percent requirement.

If parents know that they can opt out in your state, then why should they (or we, for that matter) be concerned about the 95 percent rule? Well, depending on your state, there could be important consequences related to school and district accountability standings and the students and parents themselves.

For example, the *Washington Post* ran a story on August 14, 2016, titled "Parents Sue When Third-Grade Honors Students Are Not Promoted to Fourth Grade." In Florida, certain counties have interpreted the state rules about opt-outs differently.[2] The kids in this case, honor students and some identified as gifted students were held back in third grade because their parents did not allow them to take the Florida Standards Assessment. While

ESSA leaves it to the states to decide how to determine the 95 percent requirement, the Obama administration proposed stricter rules, and others urged the administration to drop these proposals. So, depending on how the rule is interpreted, it may have detrimental consequences for you and your school.

The Education Commission of the States (ECS) provided a good summary of state-by-state rules on February 25, 2015, at http://www.ecs.org/assessment-opt-out-policies-state-responses-to-parent-pushback. To know with certainty, you should check with your state department of education for its latest policy considering ESSA's ambiguity because many states are still in some degree of flux around these issues. In early August 2016, the New York State commissioner of education wrote to the federal government asking that they relax the rules on punishing schools that are below the 95 percent participation rate.[3] *Education Week* also reported that 21 percent of New York students opted out of the New York Common Core–aligned tests during the last academic year.[4]

To guide parents properly, the core issue that educators should focus on is how the state-mandated tests are used locally. These tests should be used more robustly for curriculum evaluation and development to make the most of the time and money spent on administration. Local educators cannot wish these tests away, as they don't have much control over what the state does.

Fortunately, some states are responding in more responsible ways (depending on one's point of view), limiting the improper use of these tests. Some are replacing the high school tests with the SAT and ACT, which are probably more useful in the overall scheme of things (even though more and more colleges and universities are limiting the use of these tests in admissions—more on this in a later chapter). But many states are not making any changes and instead are hanging on to old practices. Interestingly, even in states that are trying to make their tests more relevant, such as Connecticut and New York, there exists a strong opt-out movement.

The fact is that standardized achievement tests are generally useful for making some important local comparisons, for determining basic understandings of what kids know, and for curriculum evaluation as compared to the national standards these tests are based on. Data teams need a comparative benchmark to know, with some degree of certainty (reliability and validity—terms that we discuss in more depth later), whether the core curriculum and related instructional techniques are effective. They should also want to know how various subgroups are doing compared to one another. And they may want to know that all elementary or all middle schools are achieving the same basic results or outcomes.

Being on grade level should also be an important consideration, as should knowing whether curricular interventions are having the intended impact. It would be very difficult to know any of this without some form of standardized testing. Because federal and state governments are still requiring that they be given, why not put them to their intended use? And once this is done, there is a more powerful argument to persuade parents that they should opt in, not out.

Even if local data teams, administrators, and teachers are not using the ESSA-mandated tests for these improvement purposes, they should be concerned about publicly reported accountability repercussions of having too many kids opt out under ESSA's 95 percent rule. Many states, as required by the federal government, may cause district and school accountability ratings to be negatively affected in some way should too many kids opt out. (ESSA also provides that the federal government may withhold Title I funding for districts with too many opt-outs, but there is no evidence that the federal government has ever, or would now, impose such a severe sanction.)

Because ESSA is so new at the time of this writing and the information gathered by the Education Commission of the States (www.ECS.org) referenced previously is from February 2015, many states are still in the process of determining their rules. But it is likely that there will be some form of negative accountability consequences for districts and schools when the 95 percent threshold is not made because of implied threats in the ESSA legislation.

Thus, if for no other reason than protecting school and district reputations, educators should be concerned about too many students opting out. The solution to any cognitive dissonance educators may have in promoting test-taking, regardless of what the state and federal governments do with the results, is to make sure that the local districts and schools use them for the purposes for which they were designed, regardless of how the state mandates that they be used.

THE PROPER USES OF STANDARDIZED TESTS

This discussion could apply to all tests not created locally; that is, those that are commercially developed and standardized against some benchmark, whether it be curricular, a larger population sample, or a combination of both (in the case of large statewide achievement tests, it is both). There are many other standardized tests that kids take beyond just what the ESSA and your state mandates. For the purposes of this discussion though, the focus here is on the ESSA-mandated achievement tests. In later chapters, the value of all other standardized and nonstandardized tests is discussed.

James Popham, the well-regarded expert in assessment, argues that, although there are three purposes of assessment (to compare, to instruct, and to evaluate), the more useful purposes of instruction and curricular evaluation have been overshadowed by overreliance on uses of these tests for making comparisons.[5] When thinking about how to better use these tests, Popham provides a framework, or guide, as to how we can restore a better balance. Popham's three purposes include:

- "permit[ting] us to identify score-based differences among individual students or among groups of students";
- "elicit[ing] ongoing evidence regarding students' levels of achievement so that better decisions can be made about how to teach those students"; and
- "determining the quality of a completed set of instructional activities provided by one or more teachers. These evaluations often focus on a lengthy segment of instruction, such as an entire school year."[6]

Popham argues that the aspects of testing that can be of most help, eliciting evidence about what students know and curricular and instructional evaluation, have been completely overshadowed by our country's singular preoccupation with comparison. Thus, we can see why parents are upset; schools are not using these tests for all their intended purposes. Or, if they are, they may not be making that clear enough to the public. Administrators and data teams can help restore trust in these tests by placing an equal emphasis on the instructional and curricular and evaluative uses of these tests as is typically placed on drawing comparisons. Further, administrators should make such efforts known to the public to the greatest extent possible.

THE OPT-OUT MOVEMENT: STRONG HEADWINDS

Regardless, in some places, there are strong populist headwinds buttressing the forces of those who seek to slow or shut down the opt-out movement's progress. And there are some powerful voices making these arguments. If you are in one of these geographic areas (e.g., Fairfield County, Connecticut;

the Greater New York City area [Long Island and Westchester County]; northern New Jersey; Seattle, Washington), making the case against opting out will be more difficult.

Matthew Lynch summarizes the key arguments for opting out.[7] National and state policies promoting these tests, argues Lynch, encourage teaching to the test, sacrificing means to the end, and its power in education is too broad. Without the counterbalancing actions of using these tests to improve instruction and curriculum evaluation, Lynch's points are well taken.

No doubt for all these reasons, Diane Ravitch urges parents to opt their children out of these tests, particularly common-core exams. She argues, "Opt out is the only way you have to tell policymakers that they're heading in the wrong direction."[8] Instead, she states that students should be graded by their teachers' own assessments—a position argued later in this book.

Ravitch also wants kids to have a full curriculum, making the point that these tests have caused a narrowing of the education program, edging out subjects that either cannot be tested or that teachers have little time for, as they must prepare for the tests. As a former superintendent of schools, I can attest to the difficulty of gaining strong broad-based financial support for the arts, sports, extracurricular activities, and so on in the face of AYP (adequate yearly progress) reports that were not as favorable as I would have liked in a fringe urban school district.

But here is the key issue and concern: Ravitch's position is wrong-minded because educators are not above the law, even when the law is as ambiguous as with ESSA. The 95 percent rule has been in place since NCLB to accommodate absenteeism and student transients, not as an escape hatch for those who don't like the tests. A better position would be for educators to use these tests for all the purposes for which they were designed and then help parents see the value in participating.

Should educators and parents want to see an end to too much testing, they should focus on what teachers, the school, and the district have control over, which are a great many other tests that take up much more instructional time during a school year than do these federally mandated tests. These are the subject of further discussion in upcoming chapters. But think of it this way for now: If ESSA-mandated testing takes up about 3 percent of the school year, or five to six days, why do schools administer another ten to twenty days (or even more) of summative and formative testing that no one complains about? Of all that nonmandated testing in schools, easily a quarter of it could be eliminated without much effect at all on any aspect of schooling. This book argues for such action.

ADDITIONAL RESOURCES

There are a host of resources to better understand the frustration parents have about the improper use of these tests and why more and more are choosing to opt out. The more informed administrators and teachers are about their concerns, the better off they will be in proceeding. Some very useful resources include:

"Just say no to standardized tests." *FairTest*. January 2017. http://www.fairtest.org/get-involved/opting-out. A very good summary of the key arguments for just saying "no" to the tests.

Opt Out of Standardized Tests. 2017. https://optoutofstandardizedtests.wikispaces.com. Summarizes state by state rules for opting out of standardized tests.

Kristina, Rizga. "'Sorry, I'm not taking this test.'" *Mother Jones* (September/October 2015). http://www.motherjones.com/politics/2015/08/opt-out-standardized-testing-overload. An in-depth story about the impact of testing on students and teachers.

Strauss, Valerie. "The testing opt-out movement is growing, despite government efforts to kill it." *Washington Post*, January 31, 2016. https://www.washingtonpost.com/news/answer-sheet/wp/2016/01/31/the-testing-opt-out-movement-is-growing-despite-government-efforts-to-kill-it/. Reports that, despite the fact that states and schools could be penalized for too many parental opt outs, the movement was growing at the time of publication.

———. "U.S. education department threatens to sanction states over test opt-outs." *Washington Post*. January 28, 2016. https://www.washingtonpost.com/news/answer-sheet/wp/2016/01/28/u-s-education-department-threatens-to-sanction-states-over-test-opt-outs/. Reports that the U.S. Department of Education was threatening to sanction states with too many opt-outs of standard testing by withholding federal funds for Title I.

United Opt Out. 2017. http://unitedoptout.com. A group that actively lobbies against these tests. Their 2016 national conference has the tagline "Transcending Resistance, Igniting Revolution."

What should you do? Remind parents that, as an employee of a public school system, you are a de facto agent of the state and federal governments and that you are not above the law. Neither are they. Although there may not be serious school and district consequences in the short term for students opting out of the tests, teaching kids that it's all right to break or ignore the law is not in their best educational interests. But there may also be serious consequences, most likely in penalties applied to how school accountability indexes are calculated and publicly reported.

Help parents and students know that you understand their concerns by being as informed as possible on what the opt-out movement espouses and why. Check out the resources noted here, and stay informed. Resources, such as *Education Week*, regularly carry stories on what is going on around the nation with respect to a host of issues, including national testing and the opt-out movement.

Become as knowledgeable as possible about how these tests are constructed and what they can and cannot determine, and be proficient with the various reports provided by achievement test companies. This is a real challenge because statistics are hard to understand for those not steeped in the language of numbers or properly trained. Most educators do not know all that they should about test results and reports. As difficult as it may be to learn this new language, the recent passage of ESSA clearly demonstrates that these issues are not going away anytime soon. If you are a central office administrator or a school principal, take time to learn as much as you can about the reports provided by your state ESSA test. Then, provide teachers as much training as possible so they can use the tests for all the purposes James Popham identifies and also feel more confident in speaking with parents.

To the greatest extent possible, use the tests for instructional improvement and for curricular evaluation. And make the activities associated with these efforts very public. Let parents and the public know that you value the time kids spend in taking these tests and that you are using them to improve the educational program.

USING ACHIEVEMENT TESTS FOR INSTRUCTIONAL IMPROVEMENT AND CURRICULAR EVALUATION

Truthfully, this is much harder to do than just using achievement tests for making comparisons. That's because the research methods and statistics required are more complicated. No Child Left Behind was largely focused on making comparisons between and among subgroups of students and schools, so we have ample experience with these comparative statistics (which are simple by comparison to those needed here). And from a research point of view, drawing comparisons as we've been doing for so long, while correct methodologically, is not in the best interest of all involved as we have been discussing.

Applying the correct research methodology to use these tests for instructional improvement and curriculum evaluation is likely well beyond the skills of most educators. Even if they did have the skills, they lack the time and resources necessary to properly do the job. So here is a radical idea: Use your best judgment, making sure that you do not overly attribute any one test outcome to any specific instructional activity or curricular program component. Why use judgment? Because you simply cannot do otherwise with a high degree of reliability (consistency) or validity (accuracy) without a very intense research study.

If you want proof of this point, find any good-quality, recent doctoral dissertation that attempts to use standardized test results in evaluating an instructional technique or program in K–12 mathematics, reading, or language arts. Find the methods section, and then look at the section titled something like "Threats to Validity and Reliability of the Study." Typically, this section all but nullifies many or all of the findings of the dissertation. (Most doctoral dissertations' main purpose is to have a student demonstrate that they know how to conduct proper, original research, not necessarily whether they can identify some meaningful research outcome. True, another purpose is to add to the collective body of knowledge and wisdom, but the truth is that many dissertations have more limitations than actionable findings.)

The reason there are so many threats (in terms of validity and reliability) to the outcome of the research study or dissertation is because it is very hard to isolate a singular test outcome as being completely, solely, and totally associated with a single action by a teacher or school. (This, by the way, is the same argument used by this author[9] and others as to why these achievement tests should not be used in teacher evaluation; teaching is so much more than just a student's test outcome.) To isolate a test outcome as being clearly and unambiguously associated with a particular set of instructional actions or a curriculum is extremely difficult, time-consuming, and expensive, often requiring a mix of methodologies, both statistical and qualitative. To do so "properly" is also time-consuming; requires a great deal of expertise; and, not inconsequentially, is very expensive.

So, what can you do? Use your best judgment based on a thorough discussion with your colleagues as to what may be causing a certain test outcome for a specific group of students with respect to a specific instructional approach, design, set of units, or curricular program. Having said that, if you did try something new over the course of a semester or year, such as a new approach to organizing students, a new textbook, set of trade books, introduction of instructional media, team teaching, and so on, no doubt you had a reason for doing so. And you would expect some positive result, not just in terms of students' school experiences, but in also what they know.

Reviewing annual test results in this light should provide some insights into whether you believe those interventions have had the intended impact. In a later chapter, we talk about organizing tests per some schema, one of which is the degree to which its measured learning objectives are close to or far from the curriculum. If the test outcome in question is close to the curriculum, then action is likely needed to remediate a poor result. But if it is conceptually far from the curriculum, then why worry?

But here's the catch (one of many, but the main one): *Don't overextend or attribute a singular test result in one subject area, such as mathematics, to another subject's intervention, regardless of any factors.* Just because the kids did not do as well in the math test, causing negative publicity for a school, does not mean that the new reading program is ineffective in that very same school. And, staying with math, just because the math test results were not what you had hoped for does not mean that the new math program isn't working. It may be that teachers are not properly trained and the program was not implemented properly (referred to as fidelity of implementation), or it just takes more time—two or even three years to see positive results. With this overview, let's look at each of these issues in more depth. But first, what constitutes a change in test scores that should catch your attention?

WHAT CONSTITUTES A MEANINGFUL CHANGE IN TEST SCORES?

Year to year, what change in student group test scores is large enough to catch your attention and cause concern? Conversely, what magnitude of change should be sufficient for you to conclude that something you are doing is in fact working?

It depends on a lot of factors, but first, think of it this way: Most of us took the SAT or GRE sometime in our careers. If your score varied over two or three testing administrations (if you took one of these tests more than once), would a change of just a few points be meaningful? Probably not. That's because these tests are scored on a very wide range—typically something like 200 to 800 points.

However, if you took the ACT instead of the SAT, a couple points could matter a great deal because the ACT is scored on a range of 1 to 36. Many state tests for ESSA have a fairly wide range of one hundred or more points (but it does vary, so you need to check). If your state test has a range of one hundred points, then a change of one, two, or three points from year to year probably does not mean much. The reason for this has to do with something called test error, which is explained in more detail in a later chapter.

This all gets even more complicated depending on which scores you are looking at from the test results and reports. We don't want to get too bogged down in this chapter by going into depth about various score types and their interpretations. However, one thing you can do is to check (or just ask the testing folks or your curriculum director or testing director) what the standard error for a certain test is for that year and group. *If the test score change you are looking at is within that testing error, then you are not likely looking at a meaningful change.* We are all familiar with political polls that indicate how the public feels about an issue or candidate, plus or minus some range. This is the same basic issue as test error.

Second, you should look for trends, not just a single year's result. A drop of a couple points each year for three or four years probably does mean something meaningful. A guideline to use is a three-by-three matrix. Look at the trend of scores over three years and over three cohorts in the same analysis group (such as for a school or subgroup of students in a single subject matter). If there is a noticeable trend either way, take notice, as it is likely meaningful.

Third, as discussed earlier, even if there is a meaningful change in scores up or down, don't be too quick to take credit or assign blame on any one issue or cause or intervention. The reasons for the change may not at all be what you think.

GUIDELINES FOR USING ACHIEVEMENT TEST RESULTS FOR INSTRUCTIONAL IMPROVEMENT

- The instructional intervention must have been over several months or more, not just a day or two, preferably over the entire year.
- Most of the kids in the analysis should have been in the same class or group. If there is a great deal of in-and-out student migration from the class or group being analyzed, then it is very difficult to ascribe any meaningful impact.
- The instructional approaches and interventions of interest should be significant in scope, not a minor change in what a teacher or group of teachers do. These could include such things as major changes to approaches to

discipline, looping, engaging students in taking more responsibility for their learning, and setting personal goals.

- Learn about and use the achievement reports provided by the testing company, looking for multiple-year trends that can be associated with changes in instructional approaches.
- Report your findings, no matter how insignificant, regularly to parents at PTO/PTA meetings; discuss with parents when you see them at events or in conferences. The idea here is to let them know that you use the test results and value the time their kids spend taking them.

GUIDELINES FOR USING ACHIEVEMENT TESTS RESULTS FOR CURRICULAR EVALUATION

- Two forms of appropriate inquiry are determining if a recent implementation (at least one year in place) is working as planned and determining if a long-standing program is still working as expected.
- Limit the analysis to a match between the testing area (such as reading, mathematics, or language arts) and the subject being taught. For example, match up grade 3 mathematics instruction using a math book or series with the appropriate math section of the test.
- Check the instructional goals being assessed by the test to see if they match what your curriculum or textbook series covers. If not, do not attempt this analysis, as it is too far away conceptually from your curriculum to be of value. However, if you deem that it is important to do well on the test in this curricular area, then a change in curriculum or textbook series may be in order.
- Make sure that teachers have been properly trained in the use of this curriculum. This is where a lot of problems typically show up.
- Make sure that, even if teachers were trained, they are actually using it. For example, if a reading teacher does not believe in the efficacy of fluency as part of the reading learning process, then they may not be spending the time on it as you might expect. (This is a real example that I encountered in one of my districts.)
- The students whose test scores are being analyzed need to have been exposed to the curriculum being analyzed. This seems obvious, but problems can occur due to logistics. For example, if your test is administered in the fall, then kids will not have been exposed to the curriculum long enough to draw any conclusions. Similarly, if the test is in the spring and

your program was implemented in the winter, then that is not long enough to know if the implementation might be associated with a change in student scores.

- Compare how well the group and subgroups did in your analysis to how well they did the year before. A small change of only a few points one way or the other likely does not mean anything significant.
- Look for trends over a few years and over a few cohorts (three-by-three matrix discussed earlier) to make a more definitive determination of how well a program has been implemented (fidelity) or matches what your expectations are.

SUMMARY

Just because parents are opting out of standardized testing does not make it right. And as a legal arm of the state, educators should not promote illegal activity, no matter how benign it may appear. Certainly, one can understand the angst of parents as they consider stressed-out teachers and their children over these tests. But until the law changes, educators should do everything they can to ensure that these tests are used properly and fully. The truth is that achievement test results can be very useful in many ways beyond what is typically done with them. So, it behooves educators to make the most of the test results and then convey those findings to parents so as to build their confidence around the use of this time as valuable and show that these tests should be supported, not shunned.

NOTES

1. Ravitch, Diane. "Exclusive: How does ESSA affect opt outs? Part 4." *Diane Ravitch's Blog*. January 22, 2016. https://dianeravitch.net/2016/01/22/exclusive-what-does-essa-affect-opt-outs. Ravitch sought clarification from the U.S. Department of Education on the rules for parental opting out and also on the requirement that states (thus schools) maintain at least a 95 percent participation rate in mandated testing.

2. Strauss, Valerie. "Parents sue when third-grade honors students are not promoted to fourth grade." *Washington Post*, August 13, 2016. https://www.washingtonpost.com/news/answer-sheet/wp/2016/08/12/parents-sue-when-third-grade-honors-students-are-not-promoted-to-fourth-grade.

3. Burnette, Daarel, II. "New York education commissioner asks feds to ease up on opt-out rules." *Education Week*. August 3, 2016. http://blogs.edweek.org/edweek/state_edwatch/2016/08/new_york_commissioner_asks_feds_to_ease_up_on_opt-out_rules.html?cmp=eml-enl-cco-news2.

4. Burnette, Daarel, II. "A fifth of New York students opted out of this year's common core state exams." *Education Week*. August 1, 2016. http://blogs.edweek.org/edweek/state_edwatch/2016/08/a_fifth_of_new_york_students_opt-out_of_common_core_state_exams.html?cmp=eml-enl-cco-news2.

5. Popham, W. James. "The fatal flaw of educational assessment." *Education Week*. March 22, 1016. http://www.edweek.org/ew/articles/2016/03/23/the-fatal-flaw-of-educational-assessment.html.

6. Ibid.

7. Lynch, Matthew. "Three important critiques of standardized assessments." *Education Week*. June 28, 2016. http://blogs.edweek.org/edweek/education_futures/2016/06/three_important_critiques_of_standardized_assessments.html?cmp=eml-enl-eu-news2.

8. Burnette, Daarel, II. "Diane Ravitch urges parents to opt children out of Common-Core exams." *Education Week*. April 4, 2016. http://blogs.edweek.org/edweek/state_edwatch/2016/04/diane_ravitch_tells_parents_to_opt-out_of_common_core_exams.html?qs=opt+out.

9. Goens, George A., and Philip Streifer. *Straitjacket: How overregulation stifles creativity and innovation in education*. Lanham, MD: Rowman & Littlefield Education, 2013.

Chapter Three

What Is the True Purpose of Schooling?

Little in this chapter should come as major news to anyone who has been around schools for a time, especially those serving as a teacher or principal. One might ask, then, "Why write it?" Because we need to remind ourselves of the stresses we subject kids to every day in terms of over-testing. And then there is all the wasted time to consider.

The fact is that we test our students a great deal each year for a variety of reasons. Given the profession's history with accountability, it's no wonder. Teachers feel the need to justify their grades on report cards to skeptical parents or administrators who are responding to parents who complain. In too many instances, it appears teachers need to justify any grade that is less than a perfect A+. To do so, they test and test and grade based on as objective a set of data as they can (or what they assume is an objective set of data).

Taken all together, many would be surprised to learn the total amount of testing that goes on in schools. It can amount to a significant percentage of the school year, much more than the 3 percent the federal government suggests is appropriate under ESSA. And then there are the huge costs associated with all this testing, let alone the impact on kids.

Think back to the time when you took tests and quizzes, wrote essays, and did homework in just about every subject you took in school. There were times when you went from class to class in middle and high school and you had some type of test just about *every day*. And for some of us, that was well before the current era of accountability. Presently, even in the arts, we have found our way to giving tests in the name of assessing measurable objectives.[1] One should wonder how relevant a paper-and-pencil test is in music (speaking as a former music educator)!

Then there is the issue of grade inflation, where just about everyone gets a good grade, whatever that might mean. In the news recently, there have been several stories about school districts mandating that students never receive a score less than 50 on a test. Their reason is statistically sound. Factoring in one or more 0s to several other scores of 70 often yields a grade less than passing. The argument goes that kids will then give up feeling that there is any way to pass the course after one or more 0s.

Just to be clear, this chapter does not suggest abolishing all classroom tests or those that districts use for measuring learning objectives. Rather, it's intended to describe the school day and school year from the vantage point of the child. If every teacher feels a need to test everything they do in class, then we can imagine those children moving from test to test to test. That is the typical case today, so it is no wonder that some parents are choosing to opt out of the state-mandated test as just one of the many their kids must take.

Educators can change a student's school-life environment by shifting at least some of their testing practices from written tests and quizzes to more so-called authentic assessments, where students demonstrate what they know and teachers use their judgments to determine quality. Districts, too, can help by limiting the amount of grade-level and subject-level criterion-referenced testing they use for curriculum evaluation and development. There are many ways to do this that are the subject of later chapters. Districts need to institutionalize this shift toward use of and trusting teacher judgment for determining a larger portion of a student's grade.

ELEMENTARY SCHOOL

What's that saying? Kindergarten is the new first grade? And preschool is the new kindergarten? Recently the Rhode Island legislature *mandated* that elementary schools include recess, calling it a student's right![2] Have we completely forgotten that school is supposed to be about socialization as well as academic learning and should be fun? In our era of accountability and the constant need for higher test scores, we subject very young kids to a rigorous testing schedule even if they are not yet taking the tests!

The fact is, we are testing kids in elementary schools a lot. These include response to intervention (RTI) tests, reading readiness tests, math achievement tests, unit tests, language arts acquisition tests, and writing tests. Some places even have written tests for the arts!

Many schools add one or more of the commercially available achievement tests to this regimen aimed at formative assessment—those that are adaptive in nature. All of that is before state-mandated tests required by ESSA (although, in some cases, these tests are used for more than one purpose, such as RTI, thus there is some overlap, which is a good thing). Finally, add to all this the everyday written tests that teachers utilize in their classes, and it is easy to see that there is a lot of testing going on.

The federal government recently announced that a child should not be subjected to assessments for more than about 3 percent of the instructional year. But think about that a moment: The feds are talking about the ESSA-mandated tests. A typical school year is 180 days long, give or take a few. Three percent of that is 5.4 days. Most state-required tests under ESSA take about that amount of time, some a bit less.

True, most of these tests are administered in the morning, but one must wonder how much valuable education goes on during those afternoons, with so many kids exhausted intellectually and emotionally after taking these exams. Those who have spent time in schools know that the ESSA/Common Core tests (and NCLB tests prior) are disruptive to the school day for a host of reasons. Even if the test itself does not take a full day, which they often do not, the school workflow is disrupted during this testing time.

Let's not forget all the time taken in preparation for these high-stakes tests. If we now add in all the additional testing that is conducted in a typical elementary school per year, it amounts to a lot more than 3 percent. In many cases, it can be upward of 10 percent when we factor in what teachers do each day and what many districts require for curricular evaluation beyond use of the state-mandated ESSA tests. At 10 percent, that is a full eighteen days. Even at 5 percent, it amounts to nine days!

There has also been a shift in how elementary schools grade students on report cards, moving from numeric grades to letter grades to statements of accomplishment. This shift is admirable because schools should not be labeling very young children as failures or putting them on some sliding scale of good to poor. However, the clear majority of supporting evidence for those new standards-based grades is often the same old practices of tests (and measurement) in some traditional, formal manner.

UPPER ELEMENTARY, MIDDLE, AND HIGH SCHOOL: THE IMPACT OF DEPARTMENTALIZATION

As kids move higher in the grades, they encounter more departmentalization, which means more specialized instruction and more separate testing in each subject. This is where the total amount of testing kids experience can balloon. As instruction moves from an integrated, self-contained classroom in the early grades, where kids typically have just one teacher, to the upper-elementary levels, where instruction is handed over to several teachers who have specialized training and certifications, each of those teachers now must give some form of class grade quarterly.

Each of these teachers needs to know how well they are doing instructionally and what kids have learned prior to quarterly grading, so they administer various forms of formative assessment (although they may not call it such, opting instead for terms like *quizzes*, *short writing assignments*, and the like). Most district-wide and school-wide assessment audits fail to capture this detailed information. But this is where the greatest impact can be made in reducing the amount of testing that children experience. If more teachers would substitute authentic or performance tasks for just some of their summative testing and if just a few teachers could do more with interdisciplinary instruction through cooperative planning and coordination of content (easiest to do by matching math and science teachers and then social studies with language arts teachers), then the total amount of traditional testing can be reduced by quite a bit.

MIDTERM AND FINAL EXAMS

Many middle schools and most high schools still use midterm and final exams. Here is a thought experiment or, if you are up to it, an actual experiment: How many kids received a substantially different grade on a midterm or final exam than they received during the prior semester or year for any one course on their quarterly report cards? If you want to know, then take your numeric grades (or letter grades converted to a number) and compare midterms with the prior two quarters or final exams to all four quarters.

My own experience tells me that there will be very little difference. If there is very little or no difference, then why devote all that instructional time and effort to these exams? If there is a significant difference, then something else must have gone wrong along the way because kids should not perform in a vastly different way on an end-of-course test than during the course itself! In either case, it is hard to justify continuing midterm and final exams.

Some will say that midterm and final exams prepare kids for the realities of life and higher education. The argument goes that they need to demonstrate knowledge or content under real-life testing conditions. While that is certainly true and is a valid purpose, it is hard to justify so much school time being allocated for this purpose. A better idea would be to reduce the number of days of these tests and not test every student in every subject every time midterms and finals come around.

In the field of survey science, we call this population sampling, and we would do ourselves and our kids a great service by staggering the number of tests they must take across years and subjects, thereby reducing the time required. A sampling or staggered approach could cut the amount of time devoted to midterms and finals by half!

Most of these exam schedules are typically set up by period over four days. A simple solution is to test just two days at midterms for half the periods and two days at finals for the remaining periods. This is not a perfect solution, as not all classes will be tested over the course of a year and some semester courses will not be tested at all. But experience shows that students basically get the same grade on these tests as during the regular marking periods. So, to save precious instructional time, this is an easy tradeoff to make.

There is another reason kids may not do as well on the midterm or final as during the course itself (or conversely why they seem to score the same but may not truly know the content). This has to do with how accurate the test is in measuring what was truly important about the subject matter covered. The main concepts here are test validity and reliability—issues that are discussed in a later chapter. Suffice it to say that, at this point, many of these tests may very well be weak in terms of their usefulness in measuring what is important. This is more reason to place a lower emphasis on these forms of summative assessment.

How much difference would it make if we cut back on midterm and final exams? A lot. Most schools devote four days in the winter and four days in the spring to these tests. (True, some schools are eliminating midterms, but they still devote four days to finals.) Eight days for these tests amounts to 4.4 percent of a 180-day school year! Remember that the feds are urging no more than 3 percent of the school year be devoted to tests—and they mean the ESSA-mandated tests. Between ESSA, midterms, and finals, many schools are devoting 7 percent of the year to summative tests *before* we talk about any other form of district, school, or teacher tests!

Now let's pile on consideration of quarterly grading requirements for these separate subjects. You know where this is going, right? Each teacher has to administer several summative tests each quarter so as to give justifiable grades for each student on the report card. Suppose each only administers one summative test every two to three weeks, taking up a full forty-five- to sixty-minute period. Most school quarters are ten weeks long, so each teacher is likely going to administer around three or four summative-type tests per quarter. Think of it in terms of instructional time: If a class meets every day over ten weeks, then it meets fifty times. These summative tests then utilize around 6 to 8 percent of that time!

If the same thing happens in each quarter and in all classes (this is a generalization but close to accurate), then 6 to 8 percent of instructional time is devoted to summative testing for grading—across the board! Add just 6 percent to the 4 percent for midterm and final exams, and we are up to 10 percent of the school year! Add in ESSA, and we are up to 13 percent. And we have yet to talk about all the other forms of assessment kids take each year.

We need to find a way to cut back on at least some of this testing. A reduction of even 25 percent will make a big difference, reducing that 13 percent to almost 10 percent. Cut it by half, and we are down to 6 to 7 percent of time devoted to summative testing that the school and teachers have control over. How many days does that amount to? Well, recapturing 7 percent of the school year for instruction amounts to adding 12.6 days (based on a 180-day school year)! That is indeed a lot.

WHAT IS THE PURPOSE OF AN ASSESSMENT AUDIT?

We all know what an assessment audit is, but if audits had been successful at helping policy makers reduce the amount of testing, then why do we still have so much of it going on in our schools? Is doing an audit a sort of cathartic experience? A required exercise to say that it was done? Is it just one of those projects run by a committee that issues a report that sits on the shelf? It would appear that all of the above is true, but we can and should do better.

There is only one way to get at how much testing each child experiences every school year—by adding it all up through conducting a more comprehensive assessment audit of some form. But most assessment audits do not go far enough to capture the right information. They typically focus on the big achievement and diagnostic tests given each year, often not asking all the right questions. It's easy to fall into this trap, as most of us have over the years of living in an assessment era brought on by the accountability movements of the late 1990s. Only recently have some realized the negative impact that all this testing has had on kids, parents, and schools.

Figures 3.1 and 3.2 show two very good examples of the types of assessment audits typically conducted. Figure 3.1 shows a relatively straightforward example for 2015 for grades 1 to 6 of an Ohio district.[3] It does not appear to be overly burdensome in terms of the numbers of assessments administered. Another example that focuses on RTI for second grade can be seen here in figure 3.2 from a New York district.[4] This district has a similar chart for all grades.

Regardless of focus, these are two very good examples, but they could go a lot further. If you do a quick search of the Internet, you will find others that are even more in-depth and include many more assessments, especially for curriculum benchmarks and the like, but still, most do not include what teachers are doing with summative assessment for grading purposes. If your district has already conducted one of these audits, then review it and decide how much time is allotted to *all* testing over a single school year—including what is used for curriculum evaluation or benchmarking and what teachers use for grading.

Audits that include district requirements for curriculum or Common Core evaluation can reveal a lot more testing than those shown in figures 3.1 and 3.2. Of course, doing so is a much more comprehensive auditing process, requiring additional time, effort, and resources. Many of these additional assessments are generated by the districts themselves, regional service centers, and trade and textbook companies in reading, language arts, and mathematics as part of a large-scale acquisition.

The question then becomes, "What is the purpose of the assessment audit?" If it is simply to catalogue the major assessments for planning and administration purposes, then the examples shown in figures 3.1 and 3.2 are fine, and there is a place for this to ensure important gaps are filled or duplicative testing is eliminated. But if the purpose is to *identify all the tests kids experience in a school year*—to see this from their perspective—then the assessment audit needs to go further. All tests, no matter what they are called, need to be included.

Summary Assessment Chart

	KRA	Elementary Diagnostics	AIMSweb	OGT	Ohio's State Tests	TerraNova/Inview	ELPA21	AASCD	PSAT	AP
K	X	X	X				X			
1		X	X				X			
2		X	X			X	X			
3		X	X		X	X	X	X		
4			X		X		X	X		
5			X		X		X	X		
6					X	X	X	X		

Tests administered and how they are used in this district include:
- KRA: Kindergarten Readiness Assessment
- Elementary Diagnosis (AIMSweb is used for Elementary Diagnosis)
- AIMSweb: universal screener
- Ohio's State Tests: major subject area tests for ESSA and also science and social studies at certain grades
- TerraNova/Inview: used for gifted identification
- ELPA21: "The ELPA21 fulfills the state and federal requirement to annually assess K-12 students who are Limited English Proficient (LEP) and measures their English language proficiency."
- AASCD: "The AASCD is given to students who, per their IEP, are to take an alternate assessment of the required state testing."

Figure 3.1.   Elementary assessment audit from Olentangy Local School District, Ohio, 2015.

The audit also needs to add questions focusing on the degree to which teachers *actually use the results*. For example, how have they modified instruction? What have curriculum data teams done with the results to modify content coverage? If the answer to these questions is little or nothing, then one must ask, "Why are they continuing to use them?" To get around to the actual process of systematically and thoughtfully reducing the amount of testing, a more comprehensive auditing process should be undertaken, maybe just one grade at a time or even one grade in one school at a time as a pilot project.

Grade	Assessment Tool	Purpose	Concepts of Print	Phonological Awareness	Word Recognition	Spelling Development	Reading Fluency	Conceptual Vocabulary	Comprehension	Writing Process	Motivation/Attitudes	Other	Frequency of Administration	Staff Adequately Trained?
SECOND GRADE	DIBELS	■ Screening / ☐ Diagnostic / ☐ Progress Monitoring / ☐ Outcome					x						Fall	■ yes / ☐ no
	Informal Phonics Test	☐ Screening / ■ Diagnostic / ☐ Progress Monitoring / ☐ Outcome			x	x							Fall / Spring / For at risk students	■ yes / ☐ no
	Informal Phonological Awareness Test	☐ Screening / ■ Diagnostic / ☐ Progress Monitoring / ☐ Outcome		x									Fall / Spring / For at risk students	■ yes / ☐ no
	DIBELS Progress Monitoring	☐ Screening / ☐ Diagnostic / ■ Progress Monitoring / ☐ Outcome					x						Bi-weekly for intensive students / Monthly for strategic students	■ yes / ☐ no
	DIBELS	☐ Screening / ☐ Diagnostic / ☐ Progress Monitoring / ■ Outcome					x						Spring	■ yes / ☐ no
	Gray Oral Reading Assessment	☐ Screening / ■ Diagnostic / ☐ Progress Monitoring / ☐ Outcome					x		x				One time per year for students making minimal progress	■ yes / ☐ no
	Grade Dolch Word List	☐ Screening / ■ Diagnostic / ☐ Progress Monitoring / ☐ Outcome			x								As needed	■ yes / ☐ no
	Woodcock Diagnostic Reading	☐ Screening / ■ Diagnostic				x	x		x				As needed	■ yes

Assessments used in this district in second for RTI include:
- DIBELS
- Informal Phonics Test
- Informal Phonological Awareness Test
- Gray Oral Reading Assessment
- Grade Dolch Word List
- Woodcock Diagnostic Reading

Figure 3.2.   Grade 2 RTI assessment audit from Park Terrace/McNab-Meco Elementary School, New York, 2011.

RETHINKING THE ASSESSMENT AUDIT: THE MAJOR PURPOSES AND QUESTIONS AN ASSESSMENT AUDIT SHOULD ADDRESS

How can we begin to get a handle on all the testing kids experience so that we might identify areas to reduce or eliminate? The answer is to rethink the assessment audit. Typically, these are done by a subset or committee of teachers, who issue a report. And most audits do not address the assessments teachers give in their classes, nor do they entertain the idea of cutting back on or eliminating altogether midterm and final exams.

Try to engage all teachers in the audit process. All teachers should be involved in some active role of this process because that is the most effective route to change. When adults have an active role in a change process, they are more likely to act. No doubt this will be difficult to pull off logistically, as professional development time is so precious, but think of it as the way a business might approach the issue of efficiency and focus on mission.

Recapturing about 7 percent of the school year was outlined earlier, yielding 12.6 days returned to instruction (depending on level—some levels less, some more—this is equivalent to at least 6 to 7 days at the elementary level, and at the high school level it can be much more than 12.6 days), the core mission of schooling. In real terms, that is worth a great deal of money! Or, if one prefers, it is better labeled as efficiency, refocusing resources on the organization's core mission.

Again, assume for a moment the example of a school district with a budget of $100 million, with each day (based on a 180-day school year) worth around $556,000 (rounding to make it clearer). (It is true that some costs accrue while school is not in session, but the point is that everything that goes on in a school district for the entire school year has as its core purpose support of those 180 days of instruction, thus we divide the total budget by the number of school days, not the calendar year.) Recapturing those 12.6 days amounts to energizing the core mission—instruction—by an infusion worth around $7 million! Most school budgets grow by inflation each year even with no changes in any instructional programming. Let's say the annual increase required for status-quo operations is just 3 percent; that is $3 million. It's hard to imagine adding another $7 million on top of that, which is why adding time to the school year or day is both expensive and politically unrealistic.

If that isn't convincing enough, think of it in terms of one's own personal home budget. For argument's sake, let's say that a teacher-couple earns a combined $100,000 per year. If they could redirect $7,000 to improving the lives of their kids rather than wasting it on unnecessary stuff, then don't you think that would be worthwhile? If one agrees that the redirection of these resources to a school's mission is a valuable cause, then finding a way to capture all the necessary testing information on an audit is crucial so that teachers can make informed decisions about their testing and grading practices.

LOWER THE STAKES

There is an important reason surveys focused on high-stakes issues are often done anonymously. Adults understandably do not want to share information that might imperil their positions or livelihoods. But a new type of assessment audit is going to require that all voices be heard, so to help ensure maximum participation and truthfulness, there are a couple ways to proceed.

First and foremost, lower the stakes for all involved. Senior administration, preferably the superintendent, should engage faculty by asking for their help, ensuring that all information is used formatively and not judgmentally. If the mutual goal is to reduce the amount of testing for kids, then all teachers should feel willing to engage, but the environment needs to be made safe for them to do so.

The fly in the ointment here likely is issuance of report cards. Teachers arguably will feel the need to defend their grades to parents and administration (if challenged), and the more test data they have, the safer they will feel in such discussions. Their logic is understandable; the more summative tests they administer, the better chance they have in fending off criticism of unfairness or bias. So, school climate is crucial to success in this effort.

However, if this approach is just not going to work (i.e., faculty and administration feel wary about open participation), then use an anonymous survey instrument approach followed up with group discussions about the results. The following are key questions to include:

- How well do teachers and administrators understand major achievement test result reports?
- What do they do with the results?
- How have the test results affected their instruction?
- How often do they use performance tasks, and how do they grade them? Do they use their judgment supported by analysis against group-developed rubrics? Their own rubrics? How confident are they about whether the rubrics used are accurate and reflect their instruction and content covered?
- How confident are they that class grades based on performance tasks would be supported if challenged by students and parents?

INCLUDE ALL ASSESSMENTS

Most assessment audits do not include all of the tests kids take in a school year, nor do they attempt to cover all the different types of assessments administered (discussed in a later chapter in some depth). The audit should include all assessments, especially those that teachers use for grading, not just the school-wide, district-wide, and state-mandated assessments. Again, make sure to include all assessments that *each teacher administers on a weekly, quarterly, term, or yearly basis*. Do this by grade level or subject level as appropriate.

As to the purpose of each test, use several response formats, such as diagnostic, formative and instructional improvement, evaluative, benchmarking and monitoring, and summative evaluation for accountability and class grading. Ideally a balance should exist between the various forms and purposes used. Include how much time each test takes to administer, and tally by the number of minutes by grade level. The reason for this is to see how the total of all these assessments affects each child. Because almost all schools today are still organized by grade level, this is the easiest way to view all the tests and assessments an individual child is subjected to over the course of a year.

Then, tally the results as a proportion of the school year. The calculation is straightforward. For example, if the school year is 180 days long and the school day is 6.5 hours long:

- Number of hours in the school year = 180 days × 6.5 hours = 1,170 hours
- Number of minutes in a school year = 1, 170 hours × 60 minutes = 70,200 minutes

Then tally the results by grade level and type:

- Diagnostic
- Formative and Instructional Improvement
- Evaluative
- Benchmarking and Monitoring
- Summative Evaluation for Accountability and Class Grading
- Just in case, catalogue the total of all tests, regardless of type or classification. If is called a test, an assessment, a diagnostic tool, or a curriculum benchmark—if it requires classroom time to administer, then count it in the audit.

You might be surprised to see the total amount of testing that goes on in your school and classroom, often 10, 20, or even 30 percent. Further, it is likely that the larger proportion of these tests are summative, some of which are unnecessary or duplicative.

RETHINKING THE ASSESSMENT AUDIT

Figures 3.3 and 3.4 show a more wide-ranging assessment audit instrument that captures many of the ideas discussed in this chapter. Included are sample responses for each of the grade-level categories: elementary, middle school, and high school. There is no attempt here to be comprehensive. Rather, the purpose is to offer some ideas on how to capture all the necessary information to begin a dialogue among faculty and administration on how to reduce the amount of testing that they do, in fact, have direct control of. Many say that there is not much they can do about testing because it is mandated by the feds and the state. Not true! Most of the testing that kids experience in schools is directly under the control of local educators. That is a surprising fact to many.

The survey in figures 3.3 and 3.4 (or some facsimile of) would be completed by individual teachers and then tallied by grade level across all the teachers that kids might have in that grade—thus auditing from the child's perspective. Model responses are underlined in each grade-level category. Ideally, the cultural conditions would be such that risk is lowered to the point where everyone sees this effort as a win-win process for kids. Once tallied, discussions in grade-level team meetings, subject-level data team meetings, and departmental team meetings would ensue. The goal should be straightforward: to reduce the amount of testing by the school and every teacher by around 25 percent.

Let's take a closer look at these audit questions. Readers should feel free to make modifications, as none of this is etched in stone or is proprietary of any kind. The key to success is not in the structure and content of the audit or survey; rather, in what is done with the results.

1. **Grade Level.** The results of the assessment audit should be collected and tallied by grade level to view the results from the perspective of a student going through the school day and year. When analyzing the outcome to determine if changes in policy or practices should be

Survey Question	Assessment Information	Example Elementary School	Example Middle School	Example High School
1.	Grade Level	3	7	10
2.	Subject or Course	Reading Comprehension	Mathematics	Social Studies
3.	Name of Person Completing this Survey	Reading Teacher	School Principal	Social Studies Teacher
4.	Name of Assessment	Reading Series Unit Test	NWEA MAP Mathematics	End of Unit Test for Marking Period 3
5.	I Understand and Regularly Use the Assessment Reports	To a Little Extent To a Moderate Extent To a Great Extent	To a Little Extent To a Moderate Extent To a Great Extent	To a Little Extent To a Moderate Extent To a Great Extent
6.	Who is Requiring this Assessment?	Teacher School District State	Teacher School District State	Teacher School District State
7.	Main Purpose? – can be more than one	Formative Curricular-Evaluation Summative-Grading Diagnostic State/Fed Required	Formative Curricular-Evaluation Summative-Grading Diagnostic State/Fed Required	Formative Curricular-Evaluation Summative-Grading Diagnostic State/Fed Required
8.	Item Response Type? – can be more than one	Short Answer Long Answer Written Essay Multiple Choice Computer-Vendor Performance-Authentic	Short Answer Long Answer Written Essay Multiple Choice Computer-Vendor Performance-Authentic	Short Answer Long Answer Written Essay Multiple Choice Computer-Vendor Performance-Authentic
9.	Assumed Degree of Reliability and Validity?	Low Mid High	Low Mid High	Low Mid High

Figure 3.3.   Model assessment audit/survey for tests requiring ten minutes or more, page 1.

made, it is most useful to look at the overall picture from the perspective of the students who take these tests.

2. **Subject or Course.** At the early elementary level, subject matter, such as reading, language, or mathematics, is the more relevant category. It is likely that the classroom teacher is the one to complete all this

10.	Who Constructed this Assessment?	Reading Publisher	Test Vendor	Teacher
11.	Degree that Assessment is Used to Improve Instruction or Curriculum?	Low Mid High	Low Mid High	Low Mid High
12.	Describe Actions Taken for Item #11	Re-taught to several students	Not sure how to use and interpret all their reports	Most students did well on the test getting passing grades; no change is needed
13.	The Assessment Caused Me to Change My Practice	To Little Extent To Some Extent To A Great Extent	To Little Extent To Some Extent To A Great Extent	To Little Extent To Some Extent To A Great Extent
14.	Length of Assessment in Minutes?	20	60	45
15.	Could the Assessment Be Eliminated?	Yes Not Sure No	Yes Not Sure No	Yes Not Sure No
16.	Concerns/Comments about Eliminating the Assessment		Don't know enough to judge. I need to better understand what the results mean for each of my students.	Concerned over having to justify my quarterly grades to parents and administrators.

Figure 3.4.   Model assessment, page 2.

information. But in the upper elementary, middle, and high schools, the focus shifts to departmentalization by subject. In this case, it is important to capture information from *all teachers*, not just a representative sample.

3. **Name of Person Completing This Survey.** School culture and climate are crucial here, especially when collecting assessment practices on what individual teachers do in their classrooms. While the accountability movement has penetrated the sanctity of the classroom to some degree over the past decade, it is still important to let teachers know that the results of the audit will be used to help recapture precious instructional time by eliminating unnecessary and duplicative testing. Leadership must create a school culture where teachers feel safe and

secure in sharing their true feelings about all the assessments used in their schools.

4. **Name of Assessment.** It would be helpful if someone in central administration created a comprehensive list from which teachers can choose so that results can be tallied easily and accurately. Teachers can add their own tests in addition, but a centralized list will simplify collecting and analyzing the results.

5. **I Understand and Regularly Use the Assessment Reports.** No one likes to admit that they don't understand something or use a mandated assessment improperly. *But if you really want to know the value of any assessment, ask teachers what they do with the results.* If a positive culture and safe work environment has been established, then faculty are more likely to be open and honest in their responses. This is hard but crucial to the success of the effort. There is a workaround here, if needed, that is often used in survey research that may apply. The alternative is to have the surveys administered by an outside party, ensuring anonymity of respondents, who then tallies the results in a generalized manner. Then, in committee meetings, teachers discuss the results. This will not likely work for extremely departmentalized information but will be useful for more of the general types of assessments, like school-wide assessments, basal unit tests, midterm and final exams, and so on. A better process is to have an open and honest dialogue with faculty, where a positive culture of change and improvement has been established.

6. **Who Is Requiring This Assessment?** This is a simple and straightforward item that is used for tallying results in terms of tests the district, school, and teachers have control over and those they do not as mandated by the state and federal government.

7. **Main Purpose.** The next chapter goes into this topic in-depth. The idea here is to capture a general categorization for each of the assessments given. They generally break down into these categories: diagnostic (which can also be formative, but I've separated it here because of all the federal requirements for RTI and special education), formative and instructional improvement, evaluative, benchmarking and monitoring, summative evaluation for accountability and class grading, and state- and federal-required tests to distinguish between those under the school's control and those that are not.

8. **Item Response Type.** This issue may be less important than others, but it's included to determine the level of balance between the responses students are required to provide. Obviously one would hope that there are more requirements for constructed responses both short and long than there are for multiple-choice responses. But the more that we require longer constructed responses, the less reliable may be the results if a strong rubric is not used. This, too, like the previous item, is complex and is the subject of a later chapter on reliability and validity. We are looking for a balance.

9. **Assumed Degree of Reliability and Validity.** This item is included to heighten the awareness of faculty to its importance. Briefly, reliability refers to consistency and validity refers to accuracy. So, we are asking two important questions here: First, will the assessment yield consistent results from the same student if he or she takes it a few times? Second, does the assessment measure what is truly important? No assessment is perfectly reliable and valid—there are even statistical tests one can use to determine the extent to which a test is reliable and valid. But that is not our purpose here. We simply want to introduce the topic to respondents and then ask them what they think about the value of the assessment in these terms. Again, a later chapter in this book is devoted to this general topic.

10. **Who Constructed This Assessment?** This item is intended for categorization of results. Most (but not all) assessments that can be eliminated will likely be teacher constructed or made by the district for curricular evaluation.

11. **Degree That Assessment Is Used to Improve Instruction or Curriculum.** This item and the next are crucial in deciding whether to keep or eliminate an assessment. It is here where the proverbial "rubber hits the road" on this entire issue of over-testing. If an assessment intended to help shape curriculum or instruction is not used meaningfully, especially those formative assessments designed to provide feedback on how well students are understanding the content, then why continue using it? In this item, we ask respondents to rate the extent to which these tests are used. In the next item, we ask them to be specific.

12. **Describe Actions Taken for Item 11.** Like a few other response items, this one is challenging and requires a safe work environment for truthful responses. Take time with respondents to have them complete

this open response item in some detail. Very short or no responses at all indicate one of two possible scenarios: Either respondents do not know how an assessment is used in the general scope of school-wide or district-wide improvement efforts (a very plausible case), or they themselves do not use it or know how to use it in this regard. Either way, it is a very telling response as to the value and utility of an assessment.

13. **The Assessment Caused Me to Change My Practice.** To what extent did you change any of your teaching practices as a result of the assessment?

14. **Length of the Assessment in Minutes.** Earlier in this chapter, examples were provided as to how to tally these assessment results over the course of a school year. Number of minutes is the most useful metric.

15. **Could the Assessment Be Eliminated?** This and the next item reflect the crux of the exercise. Here, we are asking for a quick response—yes, no, maybe, or not sure. This item is very useful for engaging folks in dialogue about the value of an assessment during data teams and the like.

16. **Concerns/Comments about Eliminating the Assessment.** The high school example lists the most likely concern many faculty will have: "concern over having to justify my quarterly grades to parents and administrators." Grading is a very complex issue for all sorts of reasons, let alone political. If one truly desires to reduce the amount of testing used in schools, then we cannot ignore the vast number of tests teachers use for grading.

WHAT'S NEXT? WHAT SHOULD BE DONE WITH THE RESULTS?

Change is hard, so start small with a limited project. Maybe just start in one grade or in one school. Or begin in one grade in a single school as a pilot project. But they key point is to ensure that all faculty are engaged and participate in the audit and, to as great a degree as possible, in the discussions about what to do with the results. Above all else, keep the focus on the child and how all this testing affects children going through your school year by year.

Why engage all teachers? The reason should have to do with the change process. If only a small representative group of faculty engage in this activity, then it is unlikely that their report will move all teachers to action. The main idea is to use this work as a professional development activity. When all teachers engage, they are more likely to see what they are doing to kids on a collective basis and then demand change of themselves and, hopefully, of their schools and districts.

Think of this as a professional development activity, not just as a means toward an end. We need teachers to begin to see that what they and their schools do each day has a potentially negative impact on kids. When they can see it, they are more willing to engage in change. If the audit is done at the district level with representatives from each school, the activity is too far off from the daily work life of every teacher. And remember: Most testing is under the control of teachers and schools—not mandated by the state or federal governments. To realize this for oneself, complete the audit!

Finally, try to reduce the total time kids spend in testing during a single year by focusing on (1) tests that are duplicative of others administered, (2) commercial achievement or diagnostic tests that teachers do not properly use or understand and that are not mandated either by the state and ESSA, and (3) all the summative tests and quizzes that teachers use in their classrooms. Through this exercise, try to reduce the amount of total testing a child experiences by a meaningful number without sacrificing the key accountability and formative evaluation goals teachers and schools should embark on.

SUMMARY

It's a truism to say that there is too much testing in American public schools, but no one seems to be doing anything about it. Those of us who have been around testing and data-driven decision making for the past several decades know the dirty secret—that far too few teachers and administrators know enough about standardized testing, their own testing, or some of the newer types of adaptive-type tests to make proper use of the results to justify their cost and time taken from instruction.

Truth be known, far too few educators know how to interpret the many complex testing reports provided by commercial tests even if they think the test is a good one. Without proper analysis, understanding, and follow-on actions, many of the tests we use today should be dropped. Or, schools need to spend a lot more time helping teachers better understand and use them properly.

At the individual teacher level, we rarely attempt to capture all the summative and formative assessments that begin to pile up on kids as they reach grade levels where departmentalization takes over the organizational school structure. If we could help these teachers see how their collective, otherwise well-intentioned individual actions affect a child, then they might be more open to modifying their practices.

The purpose of this chapter is twofold: first, to shed light on what a child experiences daily as she or he goes through the school year taking these tests, and second, to suggest a way to get a handle on these tests and to structure a process in such a way that educators might be more willing to engage in change. The supergoal is to recapture precious instructional time.

NOTES

1. Zubrzycki, Jackie. "States move toward standardized arts tests." *Education Week: Curriculum Matters.* September 23, 2016. http://blogs.edweek.org/edweek/curriculum/2016/08/arts_standardized_tests_assessing.html?cmp=eml-enl-eu-news2.

2. Borg, Linda. "R.I. makes recess mandatory and kids couldn't be happier." *Providence Journal.* June 21, 2016. http://www.providencejournal.com/news/20160621/ri-makes-recess-mandatory-and-kids-couldnt-be-happier.

3. "Olentangy Local School District: Assessment Audit 2015." *Olentangy Local School District.* October 2015. http://www.olentangy.k12.oh.us/site/handlers/filedownload.ashx?moduleinstanceid=905&dataid=4028&FileName=Assessment%20Audit%20-%20October%202015.pdf.

4. School's 2011 RTI assessment audit for NY State. July 18, 2016. https://nysrti.org/files/documents/park_terrace/park_terrace_assessment_audit__april2011.pdf.

Chapter Four

What Makes for a Good Test?

Fundamental questions underling all testing are (1) How good are these tests? (2) Thus, how useful are they? and (3) Are the scores interpretable? That is, when we consider a test result next to a student's name, can we confidently interpret what that number tells us about what that student knows?

What about for a group or a school? In most cases, we can add test scores together (albeit it should be the right score type—more later); compute an average score for that group of students in a class, school, or district; and interpret that average as being higher or lower than the average test scores for students from other comparative classes, schools, or districts. But what does that difference truly amount to? What does it mean?

How about for individual students' scores over time? Depending on the fundamentals underlying the different versions of the test, we might be able to compare an individual student's test score with that same student's test score from an earlier year or version and interpret the second score as being larger or smaller than the first. The complications here can be daunting, though, much more so than the comparisons of one group to another on the same test. But even then, what does that difference mean? If my score goes up three points, down four, up ten, then what does it mean?

Given all that complexity, the quintessential question is, "What does a single test score mean?" Unfortunately, we really don't know! That's right: We don't know, and this challenge is the main point of this book. The fact is, most of the effort, time, and resources that are diverted from instructional activities for testing are done so in pursuit of a fallacy, a fiction. Specifically, when people try to interpret test results, they often commit a fallacy called "misplaced concreteness"—the error of treating an abstract concept (e.g., a test score) as an accurate description of reality (e.g., what a student actually knows).

To some degree, all attempts to interpret test scores fall prey to this fallacy of misplaced concreteness. Once recognizing this fact, educators can reduce somewhat the influence of this error by considering the concepts of reliability and validity. Validity typically refers to the content of a test: Do the items on a test represent with fidelity the subject that is being tested? (Other forms of validity come into play, too—more later.) For example, a test on the American Revolution would have content validity if all the items on the test referred to the events of the Revolution that were taught. Reliability refers to whether we can trust the score as a true measure of the content being tested. If a test is reliable, then students' scores on the test would be consistent if two or more different assessors graded the exam. Another way of looking at this is whether a student was to attain the same score or close over two or more test administrations.

Because no test is either perfectly reliable or perfectly valid, all test interpretations are influenced by the fallacy of misplaced concreteness. As such, these interpretations are, to a degree, fiction because they are only approximations of the reality that is a student's knowledge or level of achievement.

To make a test "good" or "better," one needs to improve its validity and reliability—or purchase tests that are already high on these scales. Improving a locally developed test is complicated because there are few topics that are so little understood by practitioners in the field as validity and reliability. Do a Google search on "test validity and reliability," and some 47,300,000 results are returned! If you go to Google Scholar and run the same search, 2,450,000 results come back. Ask educators to explain these concepts, and they will likely have trouble doing so.

The purpose of this chapter, then, is to review these concepts using the approach taken by several recent movies in explaining other complex issues, such as how the Great Recession of 2008 happened, by using plain language and examples. (By the way, for movies that explain the Great Recession, see *The Big Short*, *Too Big to Fail*, and *Margin Call*. They are all very informative!)

Quick definitions of *validity* and *reliability* are as follows: *Validity* means accuracy, and *reliability* means consistency. So, a test that is valid is one that accurately measures what it is supposed to measure, and one that is reliable is one that will return basically the same results over multiple administrations or will return replicable results over time.

If you ever wondered why commercially available tests cost so much, it's because it takes great effort, time, and resources to produce a test that is both highly accurate and consistent. True, test companies make money on these tests, but the fact is that it takes complex science and significant effort to yield a very good test. Testing companies employ many PhDs who work on all of this, and doing so is costly.

Here are some ways to explain test validity and reliability the next time you are asked.

THE BULL'S-EYE

For the moment, let's suspend the politics around guns, the Second Amendment, and all the associated issues, and just take this example on its face value as explanatory. Let's say you are a marksman preparing for Olympic competition. We affix two rifles to a steady mount aimed clearly at the bull's-eye and cause five shots to be fired from each rifle. Figure 4.1 shows the results.

In the left-hand example, we see that the five shots are spread out with only one hitting the bull's-eye. The right-hand example shows something very different: All five shots are clustered but missed the target altogether. We can see that the left-hand rifle is not very accurate, nor is it reliable, as its shots went all over the place. The right-hand rifle, on the other hand, seems

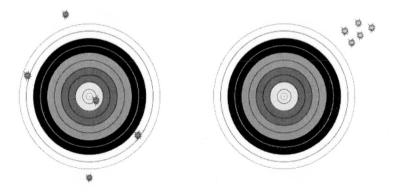

Figure 4.1. Two rifles affixed to a mount firing five shots each.

to be consistent but always misses the target. Now contrast these examples in figure 4.1 with the one shown in figure 4.2.

Figure 4.2 shows that rifle 3 was consistent—all the shots were together—but it is also accurate, as all shots went where they were aimed—at the bull's-eye. We want tests that are like example 3 shown in figure 4.2—tests that are accurate and consistent. The goal should be to use tests with items that measure what was intended (aim accurately at the right content) and consistently (return these results over time and respondents).

YOUR CAR

Another way to think about reliability is your car. You want a vehicle that starts every time you go out in the morning, even in the coldest of conditions, and one that does not breakdown after going over bumps, driving through very hot weather, or a host of other nasty conditions. You just want it to work each time, period. It should not matter who drives it—yourself, your wife, your kids—it should handle the same regardless.

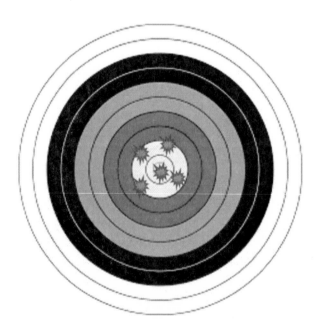

Figure 4.2.   Third rifle affixed to a mount firing five shots.

Test reliability is similar. For a test to be reliable, it should return the same basic results regardless of who is taking the test (ensuring cultural, racial, and other biases are removed) and when, such as if it is taken a week or so later due to an absence, assuming the individual took the same course and had the same information. It should not matter what their background is, the level of their wealth, whether they are receiving free and reduced lunches, or their ethnicity.

Test items need to be scanned for bias to be sure they do not favor or discriminate against any group. How could an item discriminate? Easy: if it references a description, name, or item a particular group is unfamiliar with or focuses on language usage unfamiliar or is offensive to the respondent. Then there is cultural bias:

> [I]n Philadelphia, they were giving out a standardized test to children across the area. One of the questions went something like "what is an animal that you don't see in your neighborhood? A) Dog B) Cat C) Giraffe." Well a bunch of kids got the question wrong because they lived in the same neighborhood as the zoo (in Philly the zoo is in the middle of the city, surrounded by houses and businesses and such). The question assumed that all children would not have an African herbivore in their urban neighborhood, but there was a certain group of children who did. And they would have been marked wrong because they were technically giving a correct answer, but an unexpected one. . . .
>
> Here's a real Texas TAKS test question that is a good example of bias on a test. Some students wanted to make a model to show how the size of the moon compares with the size of Earth. They used an orange to represent the moon. Which of the following would best represent Earth? Answers: cantaloupe, grape, lime, or cherry. You can argue a student should know what those fruits are. This can be hard for an English language learner, or poor students who likely do not eat as much fruit. [1]

All this concerns reliability, but how is your car an example of validity or usefulness? Suppose you buy a two-seat sports car in your twenties but then find the love of your life, get married, and have a child. Now that sports car is not that useful for your new set of needs. It is still a car that goes fast, corners great, and stops on a dime. It accurately measures up to what a sports car is supposed to be. But your needs have changed, and you don't care as much about its performance characteristics as you do about the fact that you can't put your wife, your child, and child seat in the car because it's only a two-seater! And your dog is out of luck, too!

As a married father of a young child, which car would you buy? And as a sportsman, which rifle would you want to use in competition? Clearly, it's the sedan, SUV, or minivan, not the sports car. And the Olympic contender will want to use rifle 3 in competition. In other words, we desire implements that do their intended jobs well, assuming all other factors are equal. The same logic can be applied to testing. We should use tests that efficiently measure what a student knows about the topic or content under consideration and do it consistently across subgroups.

MY BOATING TEST

Did you ever sit through a test and say to yourself something like, "That had nothing to do with the topic"? Recently, after moving to a new state, I had to take a boating safety class and exam so that I could drive my boat. My boating certificate from the prior state was no longer valid, as it was an online test. This state required me to go to the sit-down class and then take the test on-site with a proctor. After searching for every possible alternative and realizing there was no other way, I resigned myself to the task and signed up. It was a cold January day (seriously, it was really January and very cold), with snow and ice on the ground when I showed up in the morning and filed into the room with about sixty others of various ages (I was among the oldest). I told myself that, because I had PhD, I should not have too much difficulty and attended to the task at hand.

During the class, the instructor highlighted certain topics, sending a clear signal that this issue or that would be on the test later in the day. I remember one topic about transporting invasive plants from lake to lake because he gave a very clear example, and I knew that my boat was docked in a place with such vegetative invasion. During the morning, he took us outside in the cold to demonstrate the distance needed between boats before gunning full throttle (so as to not swamp nearby boats). That resonated! Then there was a discussion about colors of buoys, colored lights on the front of the boat, and direction of travel, which was all very confusing because the colors don't make much sense depending on which way you are going! He even used little boat models in class to demonstrate. I got up the nerve to ask for further clarification, admitting to not understanding. I still don't understand it to this day and likely got those items wrong on the test! Instead, I follow a rule told to me by a friend: red, right return. My friend is a licensed boat captain, and he taught me this trick while out on his boat one day when we were returning from a long cruise in some challenging waters (he was driving not me).

Anyway, when it came to taking the test itself, we had one hour for sixty questions. I kept my head down and did what my PhD training told me to do: work through the entire test, answering the questions I knew, and then circle back for the remaining test items. About fifty minutes into the test, I looked up and noticed something very interesting. All the young kids were finished, waiting in line to have their tests scored. All the white-haired folks like me were still sitting with several unanswered questions to go! Watching for a minute or two and realizing I was not likely to figure out definitive answers to the remaining test items, my anxiety grew seeing a lot of smiles on those young folks as they all seemed to be passing the test.

I waited until time was up, took my last best guesses, and then got in line to see get the result. Scoring a 93, I passed and got my boating license—which by the way is good for life and transferable to many other states unlike my previous certificate, which was not Coast Guard–approved. Supposedly I am now certified to take my powerboat just about anywhere. Don't think so!

In my humble opinion, this test was not a very useful exercise to prepare and certify me to pilot a good-sized boat (twenty-four feet with a 225-horse-power motor) in many circumstances I can think of. It's fine for my lake, but I would not take it out on the ocean, which is nearby. There was no performance component as in a driving test. True, this was supposed to be a boating safety course and test, but I just don't see how it was of much value in this regard, especially if I were going to take the boat on treacherous waterways or out to the ocean. All that could be said of it is that, fifteen minutes after a class, participants took a test and remembered enough to pass at that time. The only things that I remember are those that were somewhat performance- or experienced-based. So, this test may be reliable but not valid. (Note: I've included this section with a bit of concern that some official in New Hampshire might read this book and take my boating license away! I hereby state, under penalties of perjury, that I did not cheat on the test! But it does make my point about what is a good test.)

TEACHER EVALUATION

This is a true story. I was teaching an evaluation course in a master's program to a group of teachers in a southern state. This state, like many others, uses student achievement tests for teacher evaluation as a mandated part of federal requirements under NCLB (now ESSA, and as of this writing, it still does). But this state's requirements went just about as far as one could go in this regard. It required teachers without a direct classroom role in the areas tested, such as art, music, and psychology, to use the school average score for their teacher evaluation component.

No kidding—and I had to do all that I could to hide my incredulity of this insane policy and remain neutral in the professorial role. After much classroom discussion, I succeeded in having these students see the illogic in that policy—just in terms of test validity and reliability. Then one of them said something to me that really resonated. She acknowledged her newfound enlightenment but said that she "needed to do what was required to keep [her] job, period!" I empathized and gave up the line of inquiry.

The core issue at stake here as to whether standardized student achievement test scores are an accurate and consistent method to determine the quality of teachers is an important one. Most scholars say no. A possible case could be made for teachers of the academic areas tested, such as reading, mathematics, and language arts, but not art and music teachers using the school average! And what about consistency over time? What if a bunch of kids came to school hungry on test day? Will their test results reflect what they know about mathematics? Not likely.

Another true story: A long time ago (and it does seem like a galaxy far, far away!) during one of my superintendencies, I could not understand why middle school test scores were lower than expected. Given all the resources we had poured into that school, surely scores should have improved (this was a high-performing suburban district). When I went back to the staff and asked what happened, they reminded me about the very hot days during spring testing and noted that no one could concentrate.

I went back and looked at the historical temps for those days, and sure enough, it was in the nineties, and the heat kept building up in those rooms day after day (with no AC in the school). Was that testing an accurate measure of what kids knew that year? Probably not, given the withering heat in those classrooms by midmorning each day. Would it be an accurate measure for use in teacher evaluation assuming one could even make the case that using scores for this purpose would be acceptable practice? Highly unlikely.

WHAT DEGREE OF VALID AND RELIABLE IS "GOOD"?

Thus, validity and reliability, or accuracy and consistency, come into play when considering a host of issues, including the value of a test. But how valid and reliable must a test be to be considered "good"? My academic friends will forgive me here as I shy away from giving a technical answer (but there actually is one). Suffice it to say that no test is 100 percent valid and reliable as stated at the beginning of this chapter. There is always a matter of degree, but obviously higher is better.

Generally speaking, commercially available tests that cost a lot (and that are discussed in the next chapter) are more valid and reliable than, say, a quick teacher-made test. Further, a faculty-designed test or essay accompanied by a solidly designed rubric and applied reasonably well by somewhat-trained teachers is going to be more valid and reliable than an essay generated quickly for a unit test and scored by just that teacher working in isolation. And so, it goes.

The truth is that educators do not have the time to ensure that all their assessments are highly valid and extremely reliable. Nor should they. The point is to achieve a balance between the various assessments used. Doing so would be an unreasonable burden on their time and the school's resources. However, all the assessments used should not be those that are low on the validity-reliability scale of "goodness." When we look to select a balance of assessments to be used throughout the year, we should be considering this factor. And when we look to eliminate some testing, a good place to start would be with those assessments that are low on this scale.

In the previous chapter, it is demonstrated that the amount of assessment experienced by a student can be 12.6 percent or more of the school year (it can range from around 7 percent in the elementary to 13 percent or even more in high school). Most of those assessments are teacher or departmental creations. And, teacher-made assessments, even departmental assessments, such as end-of-quarter or unit tests, midterms, and finals, typically are not often evaluated for their degree of validity or reliability. Thus, it is likely that these are low on the scale of degree of "goodness." If one is looking to cut back on assessment, then this would be the first place to look. A second place might be commercially available tests that were instituted (for various reasons) but that teachers may not use properly or fully—a topic for the next chapter.

The next section lists several questions that are often asked on this general topic of tests and measurements. Here we get a little more technical for those wanting more information.

FREQUENTLY ASKED QUESTIONS AND ANSWERS

- **What is validity, and why is it important?** Validity refers to the accuracy of a test—the degree to which it measures the content that it is supposed to measure. It is important because a test that lacks strong validity may be measuring something altogether different from what one thinks it measures. A test may be very valid for one purpose but not valid at all for another purpose, as discussed earlier in this chapter on teacher evaluation. If we are going to take the time to give a test, then we should want it to measure as accurately as possible its intended topic or content.
- **What is reliability, and why is it important?** Reliability refers to the degree of consistency that a test or retest with the same instrument yields the same results for the same child, group, or population.
- **What does a test score mean?** Sadly, we do not know. That's the point of this book: A good deal of time, effort, and resources are diverted from instructional activities to testing in pursuit of a fallacy. Specifically, when people try to interpret test results, they often commit a fallacy called "misplaced concreteness"—the error of treating an abstract concept (e.g., a test score) as an accurate description of reality (e.g., what a student actually knows). To some degree, all attempts to interpret test scores fall prey to this fallacy of misplaced concreteness. Once this fact is recognized, educators can reduce somewhat the influence of this error by considering the concepts of reliability and validity.
- **Can we determine or measure the degree to which a test is valid? If so, how?** Yes, but there are different methods for each form of validity, and this can become complex and statistical. As for validity, the two main types are content and construct validity. Content validity is determined by bringing teams of content specialists together and asking them to weigh in on the degree to which test items cover the important content and do it correctly. Construct validity is determined by reviewing the relevant literature on a topic to determine if the construct under consideration is important or irrelevant or somewhere in between. For example, if we want to measure two-digit multiplication in kindergarten, then we would first do a review of literature to see if it is appropriate for kindergartners to know

two-digit multiplication. Probably not. Thus, we would stop right there and would not get to the issue of content validity. But if we were attempting to measure counting skills to ten, then this might very well be deemed appropriate through a literature search on what kindergartners should know. Then we would bring in kindergarten teachers and other early childhood experts to ask if they felt that counting to ten was appropriate for these kids to know, and if so, how we should ask them about it. They might say that kindergartners should know how to count higher than ten and that they should know all their numbers to one hundred. There are accepted research protocols on how to determine if these groups of content experts agree and the extent to which they agree or disagree. Next, we would ask these experts to weigh in on how to actually ask kindergartners to demonstrate that knowledge. Testing companies have manuals that can describe the processes they went through to determine validity. There are other forms of validity, but these two are the major ones.

- **Can one measure the degree to which a test is reliable? If so, how?** This is more technical in terms of statistical procedures. First, items under development are reviewed once content and construct validity have been determined. Items are then checked for bias in several areas—racial, ethnic, cultural, socioeconomic, and so on. Once this is done, there are methods to follow. One approach is a test-retest protocol to see if the retest returns essentially the same results as the first administration. Typically, a correlation statistic is run to see how stable the test is over time. Another method is more challenging, using parallel forms of the test that are not quite the same to see if essentially the same results are returned over groups and time. Yet another statistical method is used to determine internal consistency of test items; that is, are they all measuring basically the same thing?
- **Which tests are likely to be more valid and reliable?** It might be an oversimplification to say that most commercially available tests are going to have strong validity and reliability and most everyday teacher tests much less so. (I hedge here and say that "most" commercial tests are high, but you need to check their testing manuals, as I've seen examples where this is not the case.) However, considering the effort required to create tests with strong validity and reliability, it is a fair statement. When considering a commercially available test, you can ask to see their technical manual, which will describe in detail the efforts the company went through and the results. As is pointed out in the next chapter, not all

commercially made tests for a similar subject and grade level are created equal. So even here, caution must be taken to balance the end goal one has for using the test, the costs associated, and the degree to which the test has strong validity and reliability with populations like yours.

- **Do teachers really have the time to create valid and reliable tests?** No, not for the everyday tests they use. But does that mean that teachers should only use commercially available assessments? No, of course not, as that would be unrealistic. But if we are looking to scale back on the amount of summative testing children experience, then teacher judgment might be just as useful in some cases as taking a sit-down test or quiz that lacks strong validity and reliability.

- **When we say that a test is reasonably valid, what are we comparing that to? Which population or group?** There are two issues here: First, the test itself must be constructed in such a way that it measures the content intended. If that has been done, then the next question is, "For which group?" Tests generally fall into one of two categories: norm-referenced and criterion-referenced. A criterion-referenced test is one that is established against some set of learning criteria. In other words, it is used to determine if a student knows that content regardless of which group they may fall into socioeconomically, racially, ethnically, grade-level-wise, and so on. But a norm-referenced test is different. It is established to measure how a student does compared to some larger group. For example, if the typical seventh-grader knows X, then the test will be designed with easier and harder questions than what a typical seventh-grader would know about this topic. The results are reported in a way to compare a student to that group. A student scoring at the 50th percentile is said to know more than 50 percent of the population but less than the other 49 percent scoring higher. Which group are we comparing to? The group the testing company used to create or norm the test. Most tests are normed against a normal sample of students, meaning all students, or in this case, all seventh-graders in the nation. But some tests are specialized, and they seek to slice the population into narrower bands. There are tests designed to know how a student does compared to similar students, such as in high-performing suburban schools, for example, as those provided by the Educational Records Bureau in New York City. [2]

- **Are there different types of validity? If so, what are they, and how are they important?** There are many types of validity, the most common of which are face validity, content validity, construct validity, and criterion-related validity (a form of which is predictive validity). Because this chapter is focused on what makes for a "good test" in the school setting, the issues of most concern are construct validity and content validity. Construct validity is about whether the test measures the curricular areas that it is supposed to measure. Content validity is sometimes called rational validity or logical validity. In our case, it is defined as whether experts in the field judge that the test is a good one and is a useful measure of the material being evaluated.

- **Are there different types of reliability? If so, what are they, and how are they important?** Forms of reliability include test-retest reliability, parallel forms reliability, internal consistency reliability, and interrater reliability. The term *reliability* refers to consistency, or the degree to which a test will return the same results over time and over the same essential testing conditions. Test-retest reliability is simply using the same test again to see if the results are essentially the same with the same group. Parallel forms reliability is when a different version of the same test is used and then versions are compared. Internal consistency reliability is a check to see if the items on the test are returning the same results (if one or more items are yielding very different results from the majority of items, then something is off). Finally, interrater reliability is a check to make sure that two or more raters are scoring the test the same way. The most familiar issues here are in scoring high-stakes essays and in observing teachers for high-stakes teacher evaluation ratings.

- **What is the value of teacher observation and judgment?** This depends on the context and circumstances. It has been my personal experience that teachers know what their kids know! Ask just about any kindergarten or first-grade teacher, and they will tell you all you need to know about what your child knows and understands and how well the child socializes. Similarly, ask just about any teacher who spends a good deal of time with their kids instructionally, and they know. This may be somewhat less so in the higher grades, where teachers work with so many more children during the school week. But even so, most teachers know how well kids comprehend and can use the material taught. So, for everyday grading, it is likely that teacher observation and judgment are fine. But as the stakes grow higher, meaning grades become more and more important for decisions other than class grades, few teachers or schools want to rely solely on their judgment. A good example is the relative importance of third- or fourth-grade math performance in school. In many schools, how well a child does in third or fourth grade determines which math level he or she is placed in for fifth and sixth grade, which, in turn, affects which level he or she is in for middle school and then whether he or she can take algebra in seventh grade (crazy as all this sounds, it is true). Taking algebra in seventh grade is a gateway to higher levels of math and science in high school. Knowing all of this, few teachers and schools are willing to rely on just teacher observation and judgment about mathematics placement as a child rises in the grades, often opting for some standardized test as well. But the essential fact remains that teachers do have good judgment and observational skills. Thus, they should rely on them more often, substituting at least some of the summative paper-and-pencil tests they give with observations and judgments made about student performance in class.

- **How can we ensure that assessments made through observation and judgment are more valid and reliable?** Most readers will quickly know the answer to this question: with rubrics. Other than what is pointed out in the prior question, the only way to improve a teacher's rating of a student performance is to train that teacher on a set of criteria for making the judgment. We do this for evaluating student writing and essays all the time. We also do this in establishing learning objectives within courses of study. High-stakes, high school, end-of-year performances, and mastery projects are also typically judged against a set of standards or rubrics—or at least they should be. It is probably unrealistic to have a rubric for every major assignment in a course (although, interestingly, higher education is now doing this in most cases for program certification requirements), but some of a teacher's assignments, especially across a single subject or department, could be established with a set of rubrics. Essays for midterm and final exams in middle and high schools—especially high schools—should be using rubrics.

- **What are the consequences of using tests that are not of high quality (valid and reliable)?** This question gets at the main purpose of this book. Even though a test may be reliable (returns consistent results), it may not be valid (or accurate) for certain learning content for a certain group. Conversely, a test that is valid but not consistent is useless altogether when you think about it. And a test that is neither accurate nor consistent is also a waste of precious instructional time. Everyday student class and course grades (based on a range of assessments) are likely to run from low to high on validity and reliability scales. This book makes an argument for trading some of the summative paper-and-pencil tests used for class grades for a teacher's judgment. But high-stakes decisions should always be based on assessments that are high on validity and reliability scales. And even though most, if not all, commercially available assessments these days are high on these scales, if teachers are not using them fully or properly, then why spend the money and use up important instructional time?

- **What might the impact be of using a test designed for one purpose but used for another? For example, using student achievement tests for teacher evaluations or using college entrance exams, such as the SAT or ACT, in place of high school graduation tests in some states?** Since No Child Left Behind, we have been doing this a great deal, as pointed out in earlier chapters—with some dire results. If one believes in and relies on the soundness of social science research, then we should not use any test for purposes other than what it was designed for. Student achievement tests should not be used for teacher evaluation, period. There is some movement now for states to use the SAT[3] and ACT[4] in place of high school tests mandated under ESSA because states now have more flexibility in choosing which tests to use. But the SAT in particular and the ACT a bit less so have one expressed purpose: to predict how well a student will do in the first year of college. If the idea is to determine college readiness in high school by using these tests, then that would be fine. But what about all the kids who are not expecting to go to college? Should we deem them failures in high school? Hopefully not. A safer position is rather a simple one: Only use tests for the expressed purpose for which they were designed. And for all those commercially available tests schools use? Only continue to use them if teachers truly use them properly and fully.

- **Why might correlation lead to drawing improper conclusions from test results?** Correlation is a statistic that identifies relationships, not causality. We have been talking about the mistakes policy makers made by improperly using student achievement test results to evaluate teachers over the years, but other problems exist, too, as tests should only be used for the purposes for which they were designed to measure. Correlational studies should not be used to imply a policy direction that may very well be illogical on its face. Some would call this face validity, when a test "'looks like' it is going to measure what it is supposed to measure."[5] To demonstrate this point, a report in *Education Week* in September 2016 states,

In North Carolina, composite SAT test scores fell as E-rate funding increased. That led the researchers to suggest that districts aren't getting the
return on investment that they should from spending thousands of dollars
on added technology in their classrooms. "The argument that was made to
increase the [E-rate] funding up to $4 billion per year was that there was a
positive outcome," said Thomas Hazlett, a professor of economics at Clemson and one of the study's authors. "We need to show increased test scores
to be able to support the next $4 billion of investments." But suggesting
that the districts are not getting a valuable return on investment based
solely on SAT scores is a conclusion full of problems, several experts
said.[6]

   The implication here is that spending money on technology will have a
direct impact on SAT scores—a causal relationship. But the study was
correlational: "The research—conducted by scholars at Clemson University's Department of Economics and the Georgetown Center for Business
and Public Policy—shows no direct correlation between the use of annual
E-rate subsidies and SAT scores in North Carolina's public schools."[7]
This is like saying there is a full moon tonight, so the stock market will go
down tomorrow because we found a correlational relationship between
full moons and stock market declines! Or, men over six feet tall will have
black hair because there is a correlational relationship (ignoring the fact
that most people have black hair, which is true—you can look it up). But,
do these correlational relationships imply that full moons cause the stock
market to go down or that being tall causes black hair? Of course not. So
why do we expect that investing money in technology will have the singular outcome of causing higher SAT scores when the SAT is a broad test of
student knowledge and academic skills? The answer is simple: because
correlational research is really easy to do and does not cost that much to
perform compared to the much more complicated research methodologies
required to isolate causal relationships. So, be wary of correlational findings, and don't use any test for a purpose beyond its scope of intended use.
- **How valid and reliable are student grades? What should be done to
  improve their accuracy and consistency?** From a social science research
  perspective, student class grades are unlikely to be high on reliability and
  validity scales. But that is not the point. From a practical perspective, they
  are never going to be so, and we should not be worried about trying to
  make them more so. What we can do is ask teachers to rely on their
  observations and judgments more often than they do now. As a former

superintendent, I can see the challenges in doing so, especially when grades are called into question. So, this should not be an either-or argument, rather a shifting of the balance a bit. Instead of almost complete reliance on paper-and-pencil summative tests, shift some of this emphasis to observation and judgment. Doing so would likely build confidence in both sides of the equation. How useful is judgment? Anyone who has been called to testify in a legal case knows the answer to this question. The very first question asked is about background expertise to establish credibility as an expert witness. Teachers trained in a subject matter and certified by the state have a high level of credibility. We should work to build their self-confidence and that of parents in their judgments.

- **Why are commercial test reports so complicated?** Because statistics are complicated—really complicated. Think back to the statistics course most of you took in a master's program. You may remember that it likely started out with what seemed like a simple topic: measurement. But as you got into that topic, it became complex, with many forms of measurement and uses of numbers. There are nominal, ordinal, interval, and ratio scales, or ways of using numbers. And there are specific analytic procedures for each, depending on which scales are used. Test reports try to make their results clear through displays of tables, charts, and graphs, but history has told us that many teachers and administrators really do not remember much about all this statistical complexity; thus, the reports appear complicated, which, in all fairness, they are, unless one is knowledgeable in this area.

- **Is there a single metric that we should be using when looking at commercial test result reports?** The simplest comparison to make is percentile ranking, which tells how well a student did compared with other students in the comparison group. A student scoring in the exact middle of a group (could be locally, as in that school or in a school district, or across a state or nation) is at the 50th percentile, which means that half the group did better and the other half did worse. But don't make the mistake of doing anything else with percentiles, such as averaging them—you can't do that (for reasons that are beyond the purpose of this book—percentiles are ordinal numbers that cannot be averaged). All you can do is use them to compare a particular student with the intended comparison group. From this perspective, using percentiles is the simplest metric to use.

- **Is there any way to compare test results from two or more different tests?** There are a couple ways to do this. Staying with percentile rankings, if a child scores at the 50th percentile on your locally administered commercial test and at the 50th percentile on the state test for ESSA, then you could make a logical comparison that the two tests are yielding the same results or, more precisely, that the student has performed at about the same level on the two tests. Some schools use commercial tests to make just this comparison, hoping to use the commercial test to intervene instructionally prior to students taking the ESSA state-mandated test. There are also ways social scientists use standard scores that are more useful in analysis. If your commercially administered test can provide a norm curve equivalent (NCE) score, then your testing or assessment department (if your district has one) should get it (but it may cost more) and then use it for making more detailed comparisons across time and tests. A more acceptable method today (introduced to the field around 1999) is to use effect sizes to draw comparisons across tests. Because this is not a statistics book, the "Additional Resources" section at the end of this chapter lists resources where you can find out more about how to do these complex calculations and use the results.

- **What else might affect the degree to which a student's score is a "true" representation of what she or he knows?** Just about anything out of the norm. If it is a very hot day or unusually cold in the school, then scores could be affected. With the advent of online testing, interruptions in connectivity can affect scores, too, as noted in the Center for Assessment report,[8] which details how Internet interruptions during SBAC testing in three states in 2015 had both negative and positive effects on students' scores. Thus, the question of attaining highly reliable and valid scores that truly denote what students know and understand can be hard to achieve. That's not to say that these scores are useless; they are not. It just means that all aspects of testing development, administration, and fit to purpose need to be attended to for the best possible outcome.

SUMMARY

What makes for a "good test"? Or put another way, what does it take for us to trust that the student's score is meaningful? High degrees of reliability and validity. Even so, although a test may be high on these scales, a test that is not used properly or fully is not very good because it takes up precious instructional time to administer and probably raises anxieties among kids and teachers unnecessarily. To be more precise here, the test may be "good"—

that is, it has high reliability and validity—but if it is not used properly, then the implementation causes it to be less useful or good.

It is unlikely that teacher-made tests are highly reliable and valid from a technical point of view, and they never will be for practical reasons of time and resources. Regardless, teachers should make more use of their observations and judgments when dolling out course grades by employing a better balance of tests, quizzes, and essays (in other words, paper-and-pencil assessments) with their own professional assessments of student progress. And administrators should provide them political cover against parental assertions that their children's grades are unfair.

Finally, the core argument of this chapter as it relates to commercially available tests and those used for ESSA and state accountability is that they should be used only for the purposes for which they were designed. Further, teachers and administrators need to be better informed about how to more fully use them and the associated reports for instructional and curricular improvement. While ESSA is widening the corridor to allow states more flexibility on which tests to use and how to use them (which is a good thing), fundamentally, local schools do not have a choice in administering and using these tests. But they do have a choice in deciding to use or not to use the clear majority of other assessments in their schools. Because many tests lack strong validity and reliability or those that have strong validity and reliability are not fully utilized or understood, the time spent on testing could be better spent on instruction.

ADDITIONAL RESOURCES

American Educational Research Association, American Psychological Association, and National Council on Measurement in Education. *Standards for educational and psychological testing*. Washington, DC: American Educational Research Association, 2014.

"ASA statement on using value-added models for educational assessment." *American Statistical Association*. April 8, 2014. https://www.amstat.org/policy/pdfs/ASA_VAM_Statement.pdf.

Eggen, Theo J. H. M., and Gordon Stobart, eds. *High-stakes testing in education: Value, fairness and consequences*. New York: Routledge, 2015.

Frey, Bruce B. *100 questions (and answers) about tests and measurement*. Vol. 2. Los Angeles: Sage, 2015.

Heubert, Jay P., and Robert M. Hauser, eds. *High stakes: Testing for tracking, promotion, and graduation*. Washington, DC: National Academies Press, 1999.

Isaacs, Tina, Catherine Zara, Graham Herbert, Steven J. Coombs, and Charles Smith. *Key concepts in educational assessment*. London: Sage, 2013.

Kerlinger, Fred N., and Howard B. Lee. *Foundations of behavioral research.* 4th ed. Fort Worth, TX: Harcourt College, 2000.

Merriam, Sharan B. "What can you tell from an N of 1? Issues of validity and reliability in qualitative research." *PAACE Journal of Lifelong Learning* 4 (1995): 50–60.

Popham, W. James. *Classroom assessment: What teachers need to know.* 8th ed. Boston: Pearson Education, 2017.

———. *Modern educational measurement: Practical guidelines for educational leaders.* 3rd ed. Boston: Allyn & Bacon, 2000.

———. *The truth about testing: An educator's call to action.* Alexandria, VA: Association for Supervision and Curriculum Development, 2001.

Ravitch, Diane. *The death and life of the great American school system: How testing and choice are undermining education.* Rev. and expanded ed. New York: Basic Books, 2016.

Rumsey, Deborah J., and David Unger. *U can: Statistics for dummies.* Hoboken, NJ: Wiley, 2015.

NOTES

1. "ELI5: Why are standardized tests considered to be racially biased?" *Explain Like I'm Five*. 2013. https://www.reddit.com/r/explainlikeimfive/comments/19edyc/eli5_why_are_standardized_tests_considered_to_be.

2. "Comprehensive testing program: Grades 1–11." *Educational Records Bureau*. 2017. https://www.erblearn.org/services/ctp-overview.

3. "State testing: An interactive breakdown of 2015–16 plans." *Education Week*. March 24, 2016. http://www.edweek.org/ew/section/multimedia/state-testing-an-interactive-breakdown-of-2015-16.html?qs=states+require+SAT.

4. Heitin, Liana. "ACT scores slip as ranks of test-takers grow." *Education Week*. August 30, 2016. http://www.edweek.org/ew/articles/2016/08/31/act-scores-slip-as-ranks-of-test-takers.html?cmp=eml-enl-cm-news3.

5. "Face validity." *Wikipedia*. November 2, 2016. https://en.wikipedia.org/wiki/Face_validity.

6. Kazi, Jason. "Debate about impact of ed tech on test scores fueled by study: E-rate investments and SAT results eyed." *Education Week*. September 13, 2016. http://www.edweek.org/ew/articles/2016/09/14/debate-about-impact-of-ed-tech-on.html?cmp=eml-enl-dd-news1.

7. Ibid.

8. Martineau, Joseph, and Nathan Dadey. "Final report on online interruptions of the spring 2015 Smarter Balanced assessment administration in Montana, Nevada, and North Dakota." *Smarter Balanced*. September 2, 2016. https://www.smarterbalanced.org/wp-content/uploads/2016/08/090216_Report_Spring-2015-Online-Interruptions.pdf.

Chapter Five

How to Cut Back on Testing

Three Models

There are many different types of tests being used in schools. A quick Internet search yields a very long list. They appear in a wordle in figure 5.1. Although this makes for an interesting picture, the implication of so much testing is considerable.

As discussed in a previous chapter, although the federal government suggests that only 3 percent of the school year is devoted to testing, considering

Figure 5.1.   A wordle featuring tests given in schools.

all testing, it ranges from 5 to 7 percent in the elementary level to as high as 20 to 25 percent in high schools. Most of this testing is under the control of schools, administrators, and teachers. That is, educators have control over whether to use all these tests because only a very small percentage are actually required by federal and state laws.

If schools could reduce as much as a quarter of their total yearly testing, they could save a great deal of instructional time. This chapter reviews the various types of testing set in the context of the previous chapter, "What Makes for a Good Test?" Then, it establishes a framework to create a more useful balance among the types of testing to encourage reduction where possible or elimination of those that are duplicative or unnecessary.

A FRAMEWORK FOR REDUCING TESTING

For the purposes of this discussion, we separate out mandated, or required, testing from nonmandated testing because local educators have no control over mandated tests. ESSA (2015) institutionalizes the fact that testing will continue long into the future. Thus, required testing includes mostly tests that states administer for ESSA (formerly NCLB). It can also include reading inventories that individual states require for early elementary levels, and it certainly includes special education–related tests, RTI, and the like.

Nonmandated testing, or testing that is volitional, includes everything else. So, in the nonrequired bucket, we include all testing that teachers use in their classrooms for grading, all common tests that schools and districts use for determining if the curriculum is working, midterm and final exams that some middle schools and most high schools still use, and any commercially available test that a district or school opts to use for some reason (most of which are sound if properly utilized).

None of the nonmandated, or volitional, tests and assessments are inherently bad, assuming they are reasonably "good tests" as defined in the previous chapter. But taken together, they add up to a great deal of testing—what many would say is over-testing. *It is within this nonmandated bin that we can make reductions to save instructional time.*

Is it a test or an assessment? Is there a difference between calling something a *test* versus an *assessment*? *Educational test* is defined by Merriam-Webster as a " test that measures achievement in subjects of study." *Assessment* is defined as the "act of making a judgment about something." For the purposes of this book, it is not useful to make a distinction between the terms *test* and *assessment* because we are talking about the amount of time these activities take in a school year. We use *test* to describe some form of sit-down activity with paper and pencil (it could be computer-adaptive, too) where a student is tested on what they know.

Further, these tests are virtually all used in the act of "making a judgment about something"—that something being what a child knows (or at least we would hope that this is the case). So, whether it is called a test or an assessment, if it requires kids to sit and respond on paper or via computer, we consider it a test.

THREE MODELS

There are at least three ways of thinking about categorizing all school and teacher nonmandated testing for the purposes of making reductions to recapture time. Choose whichever one you want to use or are most comfortable with, but the main idea here is that there are several approaches to reduce the amount of testing.

One method is to consider who benefits from the test: students or adults. Here we opt to retain tests that benefit students and make reductions from the adult-benefiting group. A second method is to overlay on model 1 the issue of test reliability and validity discussed in the prior chapter to make more precise decisions, dropping tests that are lower in this dimension. Yet a third method is to consider how close to instruction the tests are and opt mostly for tests that are closest to instruction.

Potentially confounding this three-model framework is how the field uses the terms *formative* and *summative* (testing and assessment). Clearly, both are needed in any functional classroom and school. Our bias in this book is to retain formative testing and assessment and make reductions from the paper-and-pencil summative testing and assessment activities to obtain a 25 percent reduction. That is largely due to the striking imbalance that exists in schools between summative and formative testing, with the vast amount currently focused on summative.

Formative assessment that both informs (benefits) adults in the school about instruction and helps students to continue the learning process is the most valuable of all forms. But grading and comparisons are still necessary; thus, summative testing and assessment are still required to some extent. Throughout the three models proposed in the following pages is a bias toward retaining formative testing and assessment and reducing the other categories.

Model 1: Who Benefits?

A straightforward way to think about this issue is to ask a simple question: Who benefits? That is, who benefits from all this testing? We don't mean the testing companies because of course they do, but we mean to focus on the use of the test once administered. In fact, some commercial tests, especially adaptive tests, can be extremely useful to both adults and students if used formatively and to their full potential. Rather, the focus here is on who benefits most from a test regardless of type: adults or students.

Adults use tests essentially for three purposes: grading and comparing, instructional improvement, and curricular evaluation. Students use tests (at least they should use them) primarily as feedback to help them learn more. We understand that, in the world today, students also need to know where they stand and how they compare, so we are not ruling that out as a concern. The entire point is not to eliminate an entire class of tests, rather to make an overall reduction of 25 percent from among all the nonmandated testing that goes on in schools.

With that in mind, figure 5.2 shows placement of the variety of tests into a matrix. The vertical axis denotes the dichotomous choice of who benefits, whereas the horizontal axis divides these tests into the two categories of (1) paper-and-pencil or computer and (2) authentic, resulting in four quadrants. It can be clearly seen that most testing is in the lower left-hand quadrant, which is paper-and-pencil or computer (meaning a sit-down testing experience) and which largely benefits adults. Often much-maligned commercial testing is only a very small segment of this group, albeit an important one.

The goal of reducing testing by 25 percent could be achieved by focusing just on the lower left-hand quadrant, but one could look to others as well. Remember that all the tests on this matrix are nonmandated by federal and state laws and are, therefore, under the control of faculty and administration to change. Do we really need all those sit-down tests to give a student a grade? Do we really need all those midterm and final exams still used in some middle schools and most high schools?

Are midterms and final exams needed? If you want to conduct an interesting experiment, then look at students' quarter 1 and quarter 2 grades and then compare them to the midterm exam grade. Do the same for the spring semester. Two thoughts should emerge: First, if they are very different (grades

NON-MANDATED TESTS AND ASSESSMENTS USED BY SCHOOLS AND TEACHERS
GOAL: REDUCE 25% FROM LOWER LEFT HAND QUADRANT

	Paper and Pencil or Computer Tests and Assessments	Authentic Assessments
Benefits Students	Formative (if meaningful feedback is provided) College Admissions Tests Commercial Computer Adaptive (if used properly and fully)	Interviews Observation Essays Performance Tasks Exhibitions and Demonstrations Portfolios Journals Self- and peer-evaluation
Benefits Adults	Summative Classroom Tests Summative Classroom Quizzes Summative Classroom Unit or Major Tests Summative Mid-Term and Final Exams Prep for Common Core/ESSA Tests Formative Tests and Quizzes Diagnostic and Aptitude (non mandated by law) Benchmark or Curriculum or Unit or Common Commercial Computer Adaptive Commercial (Norm Ref) Standardized Achievement Placement International Comparison Tests College Admissions Tests (when used to compare schools)	Essays for Grading Performance Tasks for Grading Exhibitions and Demonstrations for Grading Portfolios for Grading Journals for Grading

Figure 5.2.   Model 1 testing matrix.

from exams), then something seems awfully wrong. Students should know the content on the exam as well as they did during the course. If not, then something is off, such as the test is not a good one in terms of reliability and validity or the instruction that was supposed to focus on certain content failed to do so. On the other hand, if grades on exams and quarters are essentially the same, then why use all that school time? Either way, meaningful reductions in use of these types of tests could be made.

Then, consider course grades themselves. How many sit-down paper-and-pencil summative tests do teachers need to assign a class grade with confidence? Can some reductions be made here? If a teacher normally gives three major tests a quarter, then cut it down to two. If the teacher gives four, then cut it down to three. And so on.

In the lower right-hand quadrant of model 1's matrix is a list of various authentic assessments that might be used for grading. Can some of these take the place of the summative tests that are eliminated in the lower left-hand quadrant?

Note that, for tests in the upper quadrants (that more benefit students), even if they are paper-and-pencil or computer assessments, we make an assumption that they are used fully and properly. There are too many circumstances where teachers and principals just do not spend enough time with these test reports to know how to fully use them to maximum student benefit. Feedback is a crucial function of learning, which is why formative assessment is listed with the parenthetical note "if meaningful feedback is provided."

In an otherwise ideal setting, schools would enhance use of assessments in the upper right-hand quadrant and reduce them in the lower left-hand quadrant. If total testing in a typical high school takes upward of about thirty to forty days (it really does; see chapter 3), then reducing from midterms, finals, and everyday summative classroom tests, plus any other commercial tests that are not being used properly, will easily yield ten to fifteen days recaptured for instruction. If some of this is replaced by authentic assessment, then that would be beneficial because meaningful feedback to students from authentic assessment activities, where they are engaged in learning, is probably among the most useful of activities in school.

Model 2: Who Benefits When Using Less-Valid and Less-Reliable Tests?

Let's now layer on the issue of whether a test is "good" as described in chapter 4. Figure 5.3 lists the same tests shown in figure 5.2 but now highlights each in terms of their probable degree of validity and reliability. This is not intended to be a precise labeling; however, it is close based on our years of experience in schools.

Figure 5.3 somewhat simplifies the issue, maybe oversimplifies, by using only three categories: low, moderate, and high reliability and validity. It also lumps validity and reliability together, but in the real world of assessment, it does not work that way if one were doing the statistical analysis. As said in chapter 4, a test can be valid but not reliable, reliable but not valid, both valid and reliable, or neither valid nor reliable! And it is always a matter of degree, not a binary choice. But for our purposes here, the point is to distinguish between tests that are generally high on these scales, low on these scales, or somewhere in between.

In deciding which tests to drop or cut back on, the ideal would be to strike a balance among assessment types (formative, summative, diagnostic, and authentic), as it is just not feasible to use only tests that have both high reliability and validity in all cases. Doing so is not the point. Yet there is a lot of testing in schools that is unnecessary, duplicative, or just not needed, such as for summative grading purposes. Reductions can and should be made where possible while maintaining a good balance.

Model 2 includes some caveats. The lower left-hand quadrant includes most of the testing used for grading purposes. It's hard to say where these mostly teacher-made tests would rate, but most likely, they are somewhat useful in terms of reliability and validity, so they are shown in normal type. If they are never reviewed, whether it be peer review or just the classroom teacher taking another look at the results to see if there were any surprises (such as normally well-performing students doing poorly on the test), then a concern should arise. Further, for higher-stakes midterm and final exams that are never analyzed by a team of common subject teachers, these, too, should raise a concern. In such cases, the tests are likely to turn out to be less reliable and valid, thus those are shown in capital letters.

Commercial tests shown in all the quadrants are shown in italic and underlined text and are highly reliable and valid because they virtually all go through a rigorous process of development. This, too, is not exact because some are more highly developed and have a more robust database of historical test scores on which to base new versions. But commercial tests are more useful in terms of their accuracy in measuring the right content and the degree to which they return stable and recurring results.

The issues here are that (1) some are better than others and (2) too often they are not properly utilized because neither faculty nor principals fully understand their complex reports. This is not intended as a criticism, just

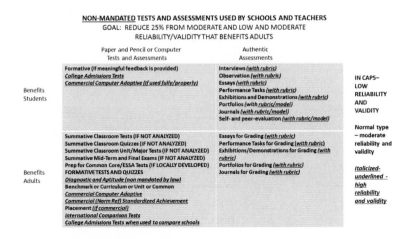

Figure 5.3. Model 2 testing matrix.

stating a fact, because these test reports are often complex. Thus, in our view, commercial tests are only useful if they are fully utilized. If not, then why waste the money and instructional time?

The two quadrants for authentic assessments include the stipulation of using rubrics, which improves their degree of validity and reliability. Rubrics are a well-known strategy for improving these types of assessment, but they are labor-intensive to design and utilize. The point is not to require them 100 percent of the time, as that would be unrealistic. But striking a balance would dictate at least some authentic assessments as accompanied by anchoring provided by rubrics.

As in model 1, most tests that could be eliminated will likely come from the lower left-hand quadrant serving the assessment needs of adults. Because authentic assessment can serve both adult and student needs at the same time and because students learn through these processes, the goal should be to move as much accountability and grading-type testing as possible out of the lower left-hand quadrant to test types in the lower right-hand quadrant.

Model 3: How Close to Instruction Are the Tests?

There is yet another way to look at this issue by focusing on the degree to which these tests align with, or are close to, classroom instruction. Logically we would want to maximize use of those tests that align closely with instruction and drop, or rely less on, others that are further afield of what teachers focus on. Figure 5.4 displays the concept.

Please note that tests that are distant from classroom instruction include standardized tests of all kinds. Final exams are also listed here because they tend to cover only a small part of instruction from an entire course.

The other dimension in this model is who benefits: adults or students? Ideally, schools would retain and maximize use of tests in the upper right-hand quadrant that (1) are closely aligned with instruction and (2) benefit students. All others (remaining three quadrants) should be subject to review for cutting back.

Is it formative assessment or testing? Most formative assessment might as well be termed *formative testing* for our purposes when that activity is a sit-down set of responses through paper-and-pencil format. If we were discussing teacher observation and judgment of student performance as a replacement for some of these sit-down tests, then it would be a clearer distinction, and using the term *assessment* in that regard would be much more appropriate. A later chapter discusses this very issue.

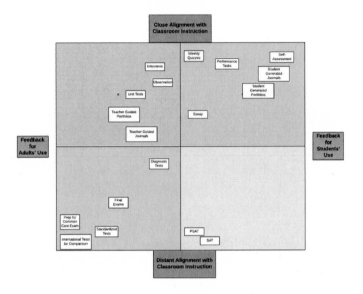

Figure 5.4.   Model 3 testing matrix.

Formative activities include observation, interviews, performance tasks, exhibitions and demonstrations, portfolios, journals, and self- and peer evaluation. These activities help maximize use of instructional time because they both inform teachers about what students know (the *assessment* definition part) and are instructional. Students continue to learn something during the exercise; they are not just responding to a prompt. True, one can learn from responding to a prompt, such as in writing an essay, and the purpose here is not to rule that out if the essay is truly meant to teach. But many sit-down essays written during the school day take on purely a summative form, as a student response on some type of end-of-unit or end-or-quarter test for grading purposes. Schools should strive to maximize the time students are active learners in school.

Many traditional formative activities are written, sit-down quizzes and tests. They provide information to the teacher; thus, these should be called formative tests. Another example includes commercial reading inventories, where a student reads a passage and the teacher judges the student's response. Is the student learning anything during this short activity? No. They are just responding. Thus, these, too, should be called formative tests for purposes here. However, an activity during which the student is actively learning and the teacher is judging, such as with observation, interviews, performance tasks, exhibitions and demonstrations, portfolios, journals, and self- and peer evaluation, is called by its proper name: formative assessment.

To confuse the landscape more so, one could make a distinction between diagnostic testing (used to determine points of learning difficulty) and formative assessment (used to gauge what a student knows content-wise during a unit of instruction). But let's keep it simpler for the purposes of this discussion. Diagnostic testing should be limited for this discussion to specialized tests used for specialized purposes, such as special education, RTI, ESL, and so on.

The assessment audit presented in figures 5.3 and 5.4 use the following general categories: (1) state- and federal-required diagnostic (to match what most schools call these various tests), (2) formative and instructional improvement, (3) evaluative, (4) benchmarking and monitoring, (5) summative evaluation for accountability and class grading, and (6) any other test requiring class time. We can then simplify that to formative (formative and instructional improvement) and summative (evaluative, benchmarking and monitoring, and summative evaluation for accountability and class grading), which leaves most diagnostic and state- and federal-required assessment in the bin of mandated testing. The overall goal is to decrease the total amount of nonmandated testing by 25 percent by making reductions in formative and summative tests, any commercial tests that are not fully utilized, and as many standardized tests as possible that are not closely aligned to instruction.

Which Model Is Best?

As one might imagine, it depends on the degree to which you are comfortable with all the test types and how much you know about reliability and validity. Model 1 is the easiest to deal with, while model 2 layers on complexities by considering the degree to which each is reliable and valid. Regardless, most testing that could be reduced is found in the lower left-hand quadrants in models 1 and 2, making that the place to start. The goal should be to reduce the amount of testing that benefits adults while retaining as much as possible those that benefit students.

It is not our purpose to denigrate all testing that benefits adults and suggest they all be cut. Nor is it realistic to think that all testing that benefits adults will be high in terms of reliability and validity. But the clear majority of testing is in this category of benefiting adults and is sit-down paper-and-pencil or computer-type tests. So, in model 1, the lower left-hand quadrant is the place to start. To the degree that you are familiar with reliability and validity, switch to model 2 in the same quadrant.

Model 3 is altogether different, as it places a premium on whether the test is close to or distant from classroom instruction, regardless of type or degree of reliability and validity considerations. While we could layer this additional consideration on top of the model, doing so is unnecessary, given the earlier discussions of models 1 and 2. Thus, for clarity's sake, we simply use the dimensions of feedback for adults or students and distance from instruction as the axes of the model.

Using this model, reductions in testing would come from the lower left-hand quadrant, where the tests are distant from classroom instruction and used as feedback to adults. But note that there are far fewer tests in this quadrant than in the same quadrant in models 1 and 2. Therefore, a second place to look for reduction is in the upper left-hand quadrant in model 3, where the tests are closely aligned with instruction but are used for adult feedback.

In summary, model 2 is a variant of model 1, while model 3 adds a new dimension of consideration (closeness to classroom instruction). Model 1 is the easiest to use at first and would generate a good deal of data-team discussion in the early stages of this process. But discussion should attempt to move toward considerations inherent in model 2. Model 3 is a more sophisticated discussion yet.

TYPES OF NONMANDATED TESTING: PROS AND CONS

This section discusses the various types of nonmandated tests schools use so as to provide more information regarding their value in the process of making reductions. Care is taken not to mention any specific test by commercial name, as endorsement is not the goal of this book. Rather, we provide a general framework and discuss general pros and cons, as no test is inherently worthless or perfect in every way.

What are high-stakes tests? A high-stakes test is any test that is used solely or mostly for decisions of promotion or retention, final grading, or placement. An algebra placement test is high-stakes when it is the single-most important indicator of whether a student will be able to take an advanced algebra class in (typically) seventh grade, for example. A final exam becomes high-stakes when it alone can primarily lead to failure of a course and retention of a grade level. Tests are high-stakes in those states where passing the state-mandated test is necessary for high school graduation. Even a teacher-made unit test becomes high-stakes when there are few other indicators of how well a student knows the material for grading purposes. When a well-balanced approach to testing and assessment is used, there should be few, if any, high-stakes tests in use.

Are commercial tests in general good or bad? Commercial tests of just about any kind, if reputable, are solid in terms of their item development (validity and reliability). Some companies have a much deeper repository of data from which to anchor test items during development and to establish norms and develop reports against. Item development is a costly task, so look to see the degree to which the company invests in teams of experts who develop draft items. Depth of knowledge 3 and 4 (DOK3 and DOK4) items are extremely difficult and expensive to develop. Therefore, schools will likely wind up balancing cost of the test versus degree to which it meets their instructional needs.

Any testing company will be able to provide their norming manual, describing the degree to which they conduct item and test development. If one desires a test that is better than another, check to see the depth of their item bank, the item development procedures used, the historical test data, and the predictive validity information on the test form being considered. To have good predictive ability, the historical data bank for norming and predictions needs to be substantial, going back many years. Regardless, one could say that all commercial tests are on a continuum of "good to great" in terms of the issues raised in the earlier chapter on reliability and validity.

The real concern schools should have about using any of these commercial tests (that are nonmandated for state Common Core/ESSA reporting) is whether they are fully understood and utilized by faculty and administration—particularly school principals. Virtually all the reports that come with these tests are complex, regardless of how pretty the reports themselves look. Statistics are statistics, and graphs are graphs. One could seriously misinterpret any of these reports if not fully understood. There is a lot of worthwhile information here but only if one understands and uses it properly.

Criterion- and Norm-Referenced Achievement Tests (Commercial)

There are many types of commercial tests available—most notably criterion-referenced tests and norm-referenced tests. Criterion-referenced tests are those that measure a student's knowledge against the content on the test. The score is an indicator of how well students know that information.

Norm-referenced achievement tests are very different, and they are called out here because of their special purpose: to compare groups of students or classes or schools to a larger population. Because most state-required tests for ESSA already provide this comparative information, it begs the question, "Why spend precious instructional time duplicating that information?" Some tests can do both (give criterion-related information as well as provide the comparatives), namely adaptive testing (discussed next), if the company database is robust enough. But administering a test whose sole purpose is to make comparisons to the national population seems unnecessary in today's world of NCLB and ESSA.

Adaptive Tests (Commercial)

There are testing companies that provide a very useful tool for schools to determine how well students know tested content. Adaptive tests are just what the name indicates: The test adapts to the student as they take the test on a computer. If a child gets an item correct, the computer program selects an item of slightly higher difficulty, while an incorrect response triggers an easier item, and so on.

Also, the number of items needed to determine whether a student "knows" the content objective is a matter of statistical development by the testing company, so look for a robust set of data on which the test itself and these computerized decisions are based. The result of this process is (1) two students sitting next to each other will have different test items, (2) two students sitting next to each other may finish at very different times because the computerized program ends the test upon successful completion or just prior to student frustration, and (3) the reports are intended to show what the individual student knows.

Some companies have such a breadth of historical information in their database that they can translate information from these tests of individual knowledge to make broader comparisons not dissimilar from the norm-referenced tests discussed earlier. Finally, it has been our experience that some of these adaptive tests are much better than others because of the amount of development necessary to produce a very good and useful tool. Care should be taken to ensure that the desired result can, in fact, be delivered by expending the high cost of administering these tests, both in terms of money and time needed for kids to take the tests. Be aware, too, that the reports from these tests are as complex or more so than other test reports. So once again, these tests should not be used because of "how good they are" if they are not fully understood and utilized by teachers and principals.

College Admissions Tests

We all are aware of these tests, but interestingly, fewer and fewer colleges and universities are requiring them.[1] And as stated earlier in this book, some states are now using them for their high school testing requirements under ESSA. If they are mandated by your state, then there is no further discussion regarding the point of this book. However, even though hundreds of colleges and universities are no longer using them, many still do, so it would be a disservice to students to discourage them from taking these exams. Because taking these tests is not typically part of the school day, the issue falls outside the purpose of this book. Finally, just for the record, these tests fundamentally have one purpose: to predict how well a student will do in their first year of college, not necessarily to test a specific set of knowledge.

Diagnostic Tests (Commercial)

Most diagnostic tests fall under the umbrella of special education and are thus required. These tests have high reliability and validity. The real concern is proper interpretation of the results by those trained to do so and to not overuse the results for purposes beyond which they are designed. Some tests could be considered diagnostic but are used for general purposes, such as tests of reading ability or achievement. These can be very useful if properly applied.

Here is an example of misuse: In one district (where I served) we used a reading inventory that measured comprehension and fluency. The fluency component is timed. Neither our director of instruction nor the reading director could understand why scores on comprehension and fluency differed to such a degree. To find out, we scheduled voluntary meetings at each elementary school and asked a set of open-ended questions on a range of topics, including this one. We learned something very important: that too few teachers believed fluency was an important component of reading; thus, they gave students more time to complete the fluency component of the test, rendering any decisions the district might make from the results useless at best and dangerous at worst!

These teachers felt badly for students struggling to finish the reading passage while being timed. Leadership then worked to persuade teachers about the importance of fluency, and one cannot say for sure whether they succeeded! The moral of this story is that proper implementation, or fidelity of implementation, of these tests is important, especially for any tests administered and scored locally.

Placement Tests (Commercial)

Placement tests, such as for algebra placement or reading placement, even if commercial and thus reasonably valid and reliable, should not be the sole indicator of a placement. Doing so turns an otherwise useful piece of information among many to a single high-stakes test.

Midterm and Final Exams (Internal)

If schools could wave a magic wand and implement changes to save instructional time, then they would drop all midterm and final exams! Realizing that doing so is not practical, schools could implement a staggered approach to testing, such as testing just math and science in the midterm and the language arts in the spring, or some variation of this sampling approach.

Experience indicates that exam grades differ little from semester grades. You can check this out for yourself just by looking at term grades of quarter 1 and quarter 2 and comparing these to midterm exams, or quarter 3 and quarter 4 to final exams. The issue is straightforward: If instruction was successful, then one would not expect exam grades to be different from class grades, assuming the tests were reasonably valid and reliable. If the exam grades are significantly different, then at least one of two things has happened: (1) The tests included topics not sufficiently covered in class (thus invalid), or (2) the instruction itself was flawed.

If the exam grades are basically the same as the preceding quarter grades, then why take up all that school time to find out something one already knows? True, taking an exam for exam's sake does have value because in life, now and then, people need to perform on the spot, so we recognize the value of these tests for this purpose. But schools do not need to take so much school time for this purpose. Cutting this time in half and using a sampling approach to schedule exams achieves this purpose and allows for the reallocation of time to instruction.

Curriculum Evaluation (Sometimes Called Common or Common Core)

Most of these types of tests are locally developed, but not all—some are provided by textbook vendors. Issues of validity and reliability are crucial here for meaningful interpretation of results. Can you imagine making modifications to a curriculum based on inaccurate information? Even if the information is accurate, how much of this is really needed to gauge fidelity of implementation? Some districts and schools do a lot of this testing, while others with inadequate resources do very little. The answer it seems is that less is more, and it would be wise to opt for as low a testing profile as necessary to gauge milestones of curriculum implementation.

Even better yet, try to use these tests for student summative grading as well. This general area is one that would be a primary consideration for reducing the amount of paper-and-pencil testing to recapture instructional time unless it is also used for student summative classroom grading purposes.

Teacher-Made Tests and Quizzes

The main theme of this book is to replace as much summative testing as possible with teacher observation and judgment of authentic assessments. But it is understandable why teachers feel a need to test often in our litigious society. To support teachers in this endeavor, training on the proper use of rubrics is important. And administration needs to support their faculty in this transition.

It goes without saying that most teacher-made tests and quizzes will likely be technically low in terms of reliability and validity, but for some strange reason society tends to accept a score on a test, even though that test may not be very good, as opposed to a teacher judgment or observation. The goal should be to begin this shift from paper-and-pencil tests and quizzes used to assign and justify grades to more use of authentic assessments, which are much more useful instructional tools. Not all tests and quizzes will be replaced, nor should they, but 25 percent is a good target to shoot for.

Authentic Assessments and Rubrics

In an otherwise perfect world, authentic assessments would be the go-to tool for summative grading purposes while teaching at the same time. Interviews, essays, performance tasks, exhibitions and demonstrations, portfolios, journals, even self- and peer evaluation (properly guided), and just plain teacher observation is a much better use of school time—if (1) some or many are supported by properly developed and implemented rubrics, and (2) the public more readily accepts these as effective assessments for grading purposes. The following chapter discusses these topics in much more depth.

SUMMARY

Cutting back just 25 percent of the total time spent on paper-and-pencil tests used for summative grading purposes (as in model 1), including midterm and final exams used in many middle schools and most high schools, would recapture a significant amount of instructional time within a typical 180-day school year. This chapter presents three models in evolving complexity for how to go about reducing testing to leave teachers more time to deal with the everyday complexities they face in the classroom. A goal of this activity should be to rely more on authentic assessments, where the process of assessing and student learning merge in the same activity.

What should school be about: learning or testing? The accountability age ushered in with the No Child Left Behind Act of 2002 and now essentially renewed in late 2015 with the signing of the Every Student Succeeds Act has fostered a measurement culture and agenda for schools that is neither healthy nor in students' best interests.

Local educators still control most of this agenda, and they can shift some of their testing that largely benefits adults to those that also better serve students. Promoting and supporting cultural conditions where teacher judgment is trusted and valued will enable this shift. No one is suggesting the elimination of all paper-and-pencil tests, as doing so is not the goal of this book. But a reduction of just 25 percent could reclaim a great deal of precious school time for instruction. And learning should be the goal of schooling, not testing.

NOTE

1. "925+ colleges and universities that do not use SAT/ACT scores to admit substantial numbers of students into bachelor-degree programs." *FairTest*. Winter 2017. http://www.fairtest.org/schools-do-not-use-sat-or-act-scores-admitting-substantial-numbers-students-bachelor-degree-programs.

Chapter Six

The Research on Why Time Matters

Lack of adequate instructional time has been a concern in educational improvement research and policy making since 1983, when a recommendation of *A Nation at Risk* was made to add more instructional time to the school year.[1] There have been many such attempts over the years since without much success. Superintendents experience excruciatingly slow negotiations aimed at adding five minutes here or ten minutes there to the teachers' contracts, making some progress at times but not enough to have a truly significant impact. While it might be convenient to blame teachers' unions for lack of progress, the truth is that they have rights to negotiate on these points, as they are legitimate working conditions that are protected by law.

The time variable has been well researched, with findings that suggest it is generally less expensive overall to add time to a day rather than add days to the year. But the lion's share of progress on this front has been in charter schools, which serve only a small proportion of the nation's school population, or, more recently, the few public schools that have been closed for poor performance and then reconstituted in some other form under NCLB. Regardless, the total amount of time added to most public school days or years (noncharter) has been minimal.

Yet, ever since 2001 standards have increased, demands on teachers have intensified, and more and more content has been added to the curriculum, the result being not enough time to do it all. Most interestingly, the research is clear that disadvantaged students benefit from more time in school, thus time can be a crucial variable in closing the achievement gap. But just adding time is an insufficient condition for improvement. What is done with that time also matters.

The research on efforts to add time to the school day or year falls into a few broad categories. Research on extended learning time, or ELT, is one classification that typically focuses on formally adding time to the day or the year through paying for it contractually—normally through some form of state-sponsored or foundation grant. But as we see later in this chapter, doing so is expensive and thus not in widespread practice other than in charter schools. Charter schools often pride themselves in providing more time for learning, both in terms of longer days and years, sometimes substantially so. But they are freer to do so contractually. One could lament this fact, but it is what it is; thus, traditional public schools have been largely unable to make progress on adding time.

A related research category is the efforts by traditional public schools to add time to a day here or there or add a few days to the year through normal contractual means such as what most superintendents and boards attempt to achieve at each contract negotiation. But progress has been slow or almost nonexistent since *A Nation at Risk* in 1983, at least as compared to the disparities with charter schools in terms of length of day or year.

The third research category focuses more on the topic of this book: how best to utilize the instructional time that already exists. More time is better, but the focus here is not on just adding time. In fact, a good deal of the ELT literature makes clear that just adding time without paying attention to what is done with that time is a less-than-useful exercise. In this regard, the long-standing research findings on use of instructional time and particularly time on task becomes important. Additional research areas include impact of added time for disadvantaged students, the costs associated with adding time, the financial condition of many states and its impact on education funding, and associated court cases.

Let's now look at what the research says about all of these issues and the importance of instructional time. The bottom line appears to be that adding time, when properly utilized, is most effective for disadvantaged students and students significantly behind.

Research on Extended Learning Time

A key recommendation among many of *A Nation at Risk* is that schools should add instructional time, as time is a crucial element of learning.[2] Since then, according to Farbman, thirty-seven states have taken up such legislation, but very few have succeeded in passing these measures.[3] No doubt, as a later section reveals, cost is the main issue.

How important is the issue of instructional time? Noted educational psychologist and researcher David Berliner, who was one of the earliest to identify the key instructional variable of time on task, likened it to other fields as such:

> The fact is that instructional time has the same scientific status as the concept of homeostasis in biology, reinforcement in psychology, or gravity in physics. That is, like those more admired concepts, instructional time allows for understanding, prediction, and control, thus making it a concept worthy of a great deal more attention than it is usually given in education and in educational research.[4]

At first, one might think this issue of time is a fairly straightforward concept, but it is not. It is entirely possible to add allocated time by increasing the school day or year at great cost without affecting learning. That's because the act of just adding time is an insufficient condition for success. Berliner identifies nine categories, or concepts, of time to consider:[5]

1. **Allocated time.** The time that the state, district, school, or teacher provides the student for instruction.
2. **Engaged time.** The time that students appear to be paying attention to materials or presentations that have instructional goals.
3. **Time on task.** Engaged time on particular learning tasks.
4. **Academic learning time (ALT).** That part of allocated time in a subject-matter area (physical education, science, or mathematics, for example) in which a student is engaged successfully in the activities or with the materials to which he or she is exposed and in which those activities and materials are related to educational outcomes that are valued.
5. **Transition time.** The noninstructional time before and after some instructional activity.
6. **Waiting time.** The time that a student must wait to receive some instructional help.
7. **Aptitude.** The amount of time that a student needs under optimal instructional conditions to reach some criterion of learning.

8. **Perseverance.** The amount of time a student is willing to spend on learning a task or unit of instruction. This is measured as engagement, or the time on task that the student willingly puts into learning.
9. **Pace.** The amount of content covered during some time period.

When schools add time to the day or year, they are simply adding allocated time. If they fail to do more, to focus on what is actually done with that time, then increasing achievement will be hard to come by.

A foundation of this book is predicated on the notion that simply adding time is not a solution, rather that shifting otherwise wasted time on unnecessary testing to a more useful purpose of providing teachers some flexibility to increase engaged time and time on task is worth the effort. But it still matters what teachers do with that time. Unless it is used for time on task and academic learning time, research tells us that learning will not be enhanced.

Originally identified by Berliner, allocated time and time on task are well-researched topics. Cotton found that allocated time strongly correlates with student achievement and attitudes.[6] Hattie, in his seminal work, *Visible Learning: A Synthesis of Over 800 Meta-Analyses Relating to Achievement*, found time on task to have an effect size of .36, which translates to a correlational value of approximately $r = .61$.[7] That is a moderately strong relationship.

ADDING ALLOCATED TIME

Unfortunately, the U.S. record on adding time to the school year or day over the past thirty to forty years has not been good and still lags behind many industrialized countries around the world. Silva found that the U.S. instructional hours per year lagged behind Finland, Korea, the Netherlands, and Japan, to note a few, and U.S. students receive on average 10 percent fewer instructional hours than students in Organization for Economic Cooperation and Development (OECD) countries.[8] Lavy similarly found a significant and positive effect of instructional time on international test scores across fifty countries using 2006 PISA data.[9]

In a 2015 review of research on the topic, Farbman states, "In recent years, a number of scholars have begun to apply complex analytical tools to identify particular practices and policies that do, in fact, generate real and lasting improvements in student outcomes. Among these, the condition of having significantly greater time than the norm consistently emerges as one of the key elements."[10] Gabrieli and Goldstein speak to the reality that kids go to school for only about 20 percent of their waking hours and that, in the final analysis, it's not just the amount of time that matters but rather how that time is used.[11] Similarly, Andersen, Humlum, and Nandrup, analyzing data from across OECD countries, find that time matters but is less effective if not properly utilized.[12]

Following this line of inquiry, Aronson, Zimmerman, and Carlos also note that adding time alone is insufficient; rather, it's how the time is used that really counts: "Any addition to allocated time will only improve achievement to the extent it is used for instructional time, which must then be used for engaged time, which, in turn, must be used effectively enough to create academic learning time."[13]

What makes for an effective school? Many things to be sure, but time well used is a crucial component. Dobbie and Fryer identify five policies from a comprehensive study of qualitative research spanning forty years that together, including increased instructional time, account for nearly 50 percent of the variation in school effectiveness.[14]

Farbman's research from 2012 identifies three points to support that "adding time can have a meaningfully positive impact on student proficiency and, indeed, upon a child's entire educational experience" by focusing on more engaged time in academic classes along with two other components: (1) more time for enrichment classes and activities and (2) more time for teacher collaboration and embedded professional development. The benefit of finding more time for embedded professional development should be of no surprise to anyone.[15] The National Staff Development Council states: "Efforts to improve student achievement can succeed only by building the capacity of teachers to improve their professional practice. . . . One of the key structural supports for teachers engaging in professional learning is the allocation of time in the work day and week to participate in such activities."[16] Further to this point, Harvard's Richard Elmore has long promoted the construct of coherence between the various components of an effective organizational model supporting the instructional core so as to better empower teachers to improve their craft.[17]

How successful are we at achieving these goals? In 2000, just prior to the advent of No Child Left Behind, Smith's research in a large urban district found that many factors came together to "cripple enormous blocks of annual instructional time," where high-stakes testing was only one factor among many (as later identified among Elmore's conclusions).[18] With ESSA doubling down now on annual testing and school budgets continually under siege, it would appear that on the whole we've not made much progress at adding enough time to make a substantial difference.

How Time Is Being Used and the Impact on Other Subjects

In their study "Time and Learning in Schools: A National Profile," Kolbe, Partridge, and O'Reilly looked at how schools with longer or extended days used time as compared to those with shorter or nonextended days at the secondary level.[19] They focused not only on how much added time was allocated but also more importantly on how that time was used. The added time was used substantially for career academy, gifted and talented, and academic assistance.

Farbman's 2015 research finds that the number of weekly minutes in various subjects at the elementary level shifted significantly post-NCLB in 2002.[20] The total number of minutes lost in art, music, science, and social studies was a whopping 243 minutes, while total time gained in math and English and language arts was 230 minutes.

In *Time and Learning in Schools*, Kolbe, Partridge, and O'Reilly found that the number of instructional hours available for science ranged from only 3.5 hours per week, or 42 minutes a day, to only 2 hours per week, or 24 minutes per day.[21] Their finding is substantiated by the work of Blank, which demonstrates the reduction in instructional hours for elementary science from 2.6 hours per week in 1988 to 2.3 hours per week in 2008.[22] During this same time, Blank reports that the time for English increased from 11.0 hours to 11.7 hours per week and for mathematics from 4.9 hours to 5.6 hours per week.

Not surprisingly, instructional time also decreased for social studies during this time period, from 2.8 hours to 2.3 hours per week. Blank notes that this decrease in instructional time for science is correlated with lower NAEP scores, "accounting for approximately 12 points on the 4th grade NAEP Science Scale. . . . States with higher average classroom time on science show a pattern of higher NAEP Science scores; additionally, states with higher average classroom time spent on *hands-on activities* have higher NAEP scores."[23]

Impact of Time on Disadvantaged Students

Of all the research on the impact of adding time, most persuasive are those studies focusing on how time well utilized helps disadvantaged students. Consistently found in this body of work and supported by most educators' experiences (especially in urban schools), more instructional time helps disadvantaged students to make up for their learning deficits, most often a result of background preparation and experiences.

Redd et al. find, in most of the studies reviewed, a positive correlational relationship between time and achievement, especially for those with traditional disadvantages, such as income, ethnic minorities, and lower-performing students. [24] In this last regard, their findings support the idea that adding time can help close achievement gaps. Patall, Cooper, and Allen conducted a comprehensive review of research on the topic covering 1985 to 2009, with similar findings that adding time is an effective approach to improve achievement, particularly for students "most at risk of failure," but only when attention is paid to how that time is used. [25]

Harkening back to the genesis of this line of research in the 1980s, Berliner notes that the Beginning Teacher Evaluation Study originally identified the concept of academic learning time as a "strong" predictor of achievement for students with low to average ability. [26] This should not be a surprise to anyone realizing that students of lower ability need more time to fully grasp the material.

And this concept is further supported by the work of the National Center on Time and Learning. Their findings conclude,

> Students in high-poverty schools with at least 25% more time outperform their peers in schools with less time. . . . Expanded learning time can raise achievement by ensuring students have more individualized learning time. Not only does more time allow for longer class periods in which students can examine topics in greater depth and in varied ways (e.g., not only dissecting a text, but also acting it out), but expanded-time schools are also able to set aside whole periods each day to focus on small-group interventions to address and overcome student learning deficits. More time also helps to ensure the inclusion of the critical classes that too often have been scaled back, such as science, social studies, and foreign languages. [27]

A key recommendation in Farbman et al. is to focus on the needs of high-poverty students when adding time. They state,

While all students can benefit from additional learning time, high-poverty students benefit the most. Data shows that families with resources are devoting increasing amounts of time and money to broaden their children's educational and enrichment opportunities. High-poverty students, however, often do not have access to the same kind of out-of-school family and community learning resources—a reality that exacerbates and widens both opportunity and achievement gaps. To begin to address these disparities, it is necessary to offer more and better in-school learning time, such that high-needs students gain access to additional educational opportunities and the individualized supports that flourish in a well-designed, high-quality, expanded learning time school.[28]

Cost Factors

The bottom line is that adding time is expensive—very expensive. And school budgets in many places are only getting tighter, making such efforts to "buy" more time unrealistic as many schools have yet to fully recover from the Great Recession of 2008.[29] This is due in part to financial exigencies facing some states but also politics. As the *New York Times* reported at the beginning of the 2016–2017 school year, "In several states where school budgets have still not recovered from the recession, lawmakers—not the economy—are largely to blame."[30]

Politics aside, money is an issue. The Center on Budget and Policy Priorities reports that most states spent less on K–12 education in the 2014–2015 school year than they did in 2007–2008. Recent spending for public education has begun to recover from its 2008 low, with thirty-four states increasing spending per pupil but still below pre-Recession levels.[31] Their report identifies four factors affecting school budgets: (1) Revenues remain below pre-Recession levels, (2) costs are rising, (3) states have avoided raising new revenues, and (4) federal aid to states has fallen. No wonder so many superintendents and board members have gray hair!

Remember that adding a day is typically costed out as an equal or nearly an equal proportion of the current number of days in the school year divided into the total school budget. (While many district employees work beyond the student school year, they do so in support of that school year; thus for making these model calculations, we lump all costs together and divide by the number of school days in the calendar.) So if the budget is $100,000,000 and the school year is 180 days long, then one additional day effectively costs $555,555 (or so—probably less, but the point is made). And adding time onto the length of the day is equally problematic in terms of cost and execution, but more places seem to be having some success here as compared to significantly adding to the length of the school year.

What does it cost to add allocated time? Silva found that a 10 percent increase in time typically requires a 6 to 7 percent increase in cost.[32] So adding 18 days to a normal 180-day school year would likely cost (assuming the earlier example of a base budget of $100,000,000) an additional $6 to $7 million. And that is before any consideration for additional federal- and state-mandated regulatory costs, building maintenance; annual inflationary costs for bussing and the like; or any number of other needs a school district will have from year to year. Silva goes on to report that a proposal by Minnesota school superintendents to dramatically extend the school year by twenty-five days was estimated to cost some $750 million and was abandoned on grounds of political feasibility.

A year earlier, Pennington also found cost a prohibitive factor.[33] Most interesting, though, is her finding that some schools are able to affordably add time to the day, and the cost to do so is somewhat less per hour than the district average cost per hour. Schools in her study accomplished this by patching together a range of financial and other supports to effectively add time to the day, or what she calls "extended-time school." But when one does the calculation of what this extra time costs compared to the hourly cost in comparative district schools, the ratio Silva identified holds here, too—about two-thirds the cost. The difference is that it does not affect across the board every school and every school day. Thus, it is likely a more affordable approach. Pennington concludes,

> Clearly, one of the great challenges of extending learning time is the cost of doing so. The schools profiled in this example have figured out ways to extend learning time without a higher per pupil allocation. They combine funds from a number of different sources, including after school dollars; summer school dollars; 21st Century Community Learning Centers; private fund-raising; and leveraging the resources raised separately by community partners. School leaders spend inordinate amounts of time patching together resources from these fragile funding sources. . . . While the success of these schools demonstrates that it is possible for determined school leaders to find resources, this is not an adequate long-term funding strategy for schools in which every student participates in a coherent extended day/year design.[34]

LITIGATION

In an effort to resolve the school funding crisis, plaintiffs across the country have taken their states to court, arguing on a number of grounds that funding is inadequate and must be increased. Typically, these cases contend that the state's funding formulas shortchange disadvantaged students or that the state's constitutional protections to provide all children an adequate education have been violated or both. The National Education Access Network reports that similar cases have been taken in forty-five of the fifty states, and you can check your state at its website.[35] The Education Law Center notes, "Even though they tax themselves at higher rates, low-wealth communities are often unable to generate sufficient funds for their schools. At the same time, state funding usually falls short, and some states even distribute funds in ways that worsen resource inequities."[36]

In Connecticut, a state that is home to two of this book's authors and thus near and dear to our hearts, the superior court ruled in September 2016 that, not only is the state's system of funding public schools unconstitutional, but it is also illogical.[37] The judge also called into question many other aspects of the educational system, including how teachers are evaluated and whether compensation should be tied to student performance, how special education is funded, and how districts are reimbursed for building aid, among other points. Surprisingly, the judge ruled against the core argument put forth by plaintiffs that the funding formula is inadequate, ruling instead on just about every other facet of schooling.

This is a landmark case of immense proportions in terms of breadth of reach, given the superior court judge's ruling, which has now been appealed by both the plaintiffs and defendants. Thus, like so many others across the country, this case will eventually be resolved at the state supreme court level several years down the line. It will be ten years or more from initial filing of the case before it is resolved one way or the other.

Given all this legal activity, one would think that schools would be better off financially, but that is not the case, largely because the legal and political process is very slow, as is unfolding in Connecticut right now. After lengthy court proceedings, courts mandate that legislatures make changes; the legislature stalls or makes halfhearted attempts, requiring the plaintiffs to go back to court some years later to seek injunctive relief, only to start the circular legal and political process all over again.

As superintendents, we have been through all of this before, which is why, after so much experience and consideration, we now seek ways to better and more affordably add instructional time to the school day. Realizing that so many nonmandated tests used in schools today are unnecessary, duplicative, or not used fully, a rational approach to finding more time within the existing organizational structure of schools is to reduce this waste and turn it into more productive use.

SUMMARY

This chapter makes clear that the basic effort to add allocated time in traditional public schools is a difficult and costly challenge. Even if it were successful (which is not the case), just adding allocated time is a necessary but insufficient condition for improving student achievement. Educators must also focus on what is done with that time to help students learn the material.

In 1985, Gettinger found that focusing on the amount of time to learn was as useful as or a better set of predictors than are intelligence measures.[38] Berliner reminds us of the mastery model, whose core belief is that most students can learn complex material given sufficient time to do so. Berliner also sums up the bottom line:

> To generalize, any proposal to change instructional materials or teaching practices in the classroom that does not affect allocated time, engaged time, the rate of success, or the alignment of the curriculum with the outcome measure that is used to assess learning is likely not to affect student achievement. The strongest statement derived from the ALT *(academic learning time)* model of instruction is that unless ALT is affected in some way, there will be no changes in student achievement at all.[39]

That was in 1990, and the very same holds true today.

If adding time for time on task and instructional learning time is so important yet there is so little progress at achieving this goal (largely due to cost), then what can be done? Through our personal experiences and reflections on the amount of time wasted on unnecessary and duplicative nonmandated summative testing for grading, curricular evaluation, and the use of commercial tests that are little-understood and -used or used improperly (which is worse), it makes sense to consider cutting back some to recapture allocated time, which can be turned to better use for academic learning time.

In summation, we have a set of research findings that are clear and a set of financial and political conditions that thwart implementation of those recommendations, and many schools waste a lot of time on nonmandated, unnecessary testing. The partial solution and one that is completely under local educators' control is a rather logical one: to cut back on the unnecessary for the really important work to continue.

NOTES

1. Gardner, David P. *A nation at risk*. Washington, DC: National Commission on Excellence in Education, U.S. Department of Education, 1983.

2. Ibid.

3. Farbman, David. "The case for improving and expanding time in school: A review of key research and practice." *National Center on Time and Learning*. 2012. http://files.eric.ed.gov/fulltext/ED534894.pdf.

4. Berliner, David C. "What's all the fuss about instructional time?" In *The nature of time in schools: Theoretical concepts, practitioner perceptions*, edited by Miriam Ben-Peretz and Rainer Bromme. New York: Teachers College Press, 1990, p. 2.

5. Ibid.

6. Cotton, Kathleen. "Educational time factors." *Education Northwest*. 1989. http://educationnorthwest.org/sites/default/files/EducationalTimeFactors.pdf.

7. Hattie, John. *Visible learning: A synthesis of over 800 meta-analyses relating to achievement*. London: Routledge, 2009.

8. Silva, Elena. *On the clock: Rethinking the way schools use time*. Washington, DC: Education Sector, 2007.

9. Lavy, Victor. " Expanding school resources and increasing time on task: Effects of a policy experiment in Israel on student academic achievement and behavior." Working paper 18369, National Bureau of Economic Research, Cambridge, MA, September 2012, p. 34.

10. Farbman, "Case for improving," p. 23.

11. Gabrieli, Christopher, and Warren Goldstein. *Time to learn: How a new school schedule is making smarter kids, happier parents, and safer neighborhoods*. San Francisco, CA: Jossey-Bass, 2008, p. 36.

12. Andersen, Simon Calmar, Maria Knoth Humlum, and Anne Brink Nandrup. "Increasing instruction time in school does increase learning." *Proceedings of the National Academy of Sciences* 113, no. 27 (July 5, 2016): 7481–84.

13. Aronson, Julie, Joy Zimmerman, and Lisa Carlos. "Improving student achievement by extending school time: Is it just a matter of time?" *WestEd*. April 1998, p. 3. https://www.wested.org/online_pubs/po-98-02.pdf.

14. Dobbie, Will, and Roland G. Fryer Jr. "Getting beneath the veil of effective schools: Evidence from New York City." *American Economic Journal: Applied Economics* 5, no. 4 (2013): 28–60.

15. Farbman, "Case for improving."

16. Darling-Hammond, Linda, Ruth Chung Wei, Alethea Andree, Nikole Richardson, and Stelios Orphanos. *Professional learning in the learning profession: A status report on teacher development in the United States and abroad*. Washington, DC: National Staff Development Council, 2009, p. 20.

17. Elmore, Richard F., Michelle L. Forman, Elizabeth L. Stosich, and Candice Bocala. "The internal coherence assessment protocol and developmental framework: Building the organizational capacity for instructional improvement in schools." *Strategic Education Research Partnership Publications, Research Paper*, April 2014.

18. Smith, BetsAnn. "Quantity matters: Annual instructional time in an urban school system." *Educational Administration Quarterly* 36, no. 5 (2000): 652–82.

19. Kolbe, Tammy, Mark Partridge, and Fran O'Reilly. *Time and learning in schools: A national profile*. Boston: National Center on Time and Learning, 2012.

20. Farbman, "Case for improving."

21. Kolbe, Partridge, and O'Reilly, *Time and learning*.

22. Blank, Rolf K. "What is the impact of decline in science instructional time in elementary school?" Paper prepared for the Noyce Foundation, 2012. www.csss-science.org/downloads/NAEPElemScienceData.pdf.

23. Ibid., p. 19.

24. Redd, Zakia, Christopher Boccanfuso, Karen Walker, Daniel Princiotta, Dylan Knewstub, and Kristin Moore. *Expanding time for learning both inside and outside the classroom: A review of the evidence base*. New York: Wallace Foundation, 2012.

25. Patall, Erika A., Harris Cooper, and Ashley Batts Allen. "Extending the school day or school year: A systematic review of research (1985–2009)." *Review of Educational Research* 80, no. 3 (2010): 401–36.

26. Berliner, "What's all the fuss?"

27. "Raise achievement." *National Center on Time and Learning*. 2017. http://www.timeandlearning.org/why-more-school-time/raise-achievement.

28. Farbman, David, Jennifer Davis, David Goldberg, and Julie Rowland. "Learning time in America: Trends to reform the American school calendar: A snapshot of federal, state and local action." *Education Commission of the States* (Spring 2015), p. 21.

29. http://theweek.com/articles/646430/continued-plight-americas-public-schools.

30. Editorial Board. "Back to school with budgets still tight." *New York Times*, August 29, 2016. http://www.nytimes.com/2016/08/29/opinion/back-to-school-with-budgets-still-tight.html?smprod=nytcore-iphone&smid=nytcore-iphone-share.

31. Leachman, Michael, and Chris Mai. "Most states still funding schools less than before the Recession." *Center on Budget and Policy Priorities*. May 20, 2014. http://www.cbpp.org/files/9-12-13sfp.pdf.

32. Silva, *On the clock*.

33. Pennington, Hilary. *Expanding learning time in high schools*. Washington, DC: Center for American Progress, 2006.

34. Ibid., p. 23.

35. *National Education Access Network*. 2017. http://www.schoolfunding.info/states/state_by_state.php3.

36. "Litigation." *Education Law Center*. 2017. http://www.educationjustice.org/litigation.html.

37. Altimari, Daniela. "Lawmakers scramble to craft response to judge's education ruling." *Hartford Courant*. September 9, 2016. http://www.courant.com/education/hc-education-lawsuit-follo-20160908-story.html.

38. Gettinger, Maribeth. "Time allocated and time spent relative to time needed for learning as determinants of achievement." *Journal of Educational Psychology* 77, no. 1 (1985): 3.

39. Berliner, "What's all the fuss?" p. 19.

Chapter Seven

High School Case Study

Imagine implementing the ideas put forward so far. What would it look like in practice? High school, with the most amount of time to gain yet, being so departmentalized, the hardest structure to reform, is a good place to model personalized and project-based learning. Achieving success will be up to each teacher's ability to engage students in performances and projects, personalized to their interests, and then find ways to test less and rely more on her or his judgment for grading those evidences.

This chapter presents such an example from the practice of a Long Island, New York, social studies teacher covering an entire semester of work in a "Participation in Government" course. The instructor is Thomas Cook, an old friend (now retired) who agreed to share his experiences, as they serendipitously fit so nicely into the reform framework proposed in this book.[1]

Three main constructs—or ideas—underpin the value of this case study example: the use of formative assessment, the value of teacher judgment in assessment, and the importance of personalized learning to engage students. Earlier chapters discuss the purpose and use of formative assessment, thus there is no need to repeat that here. Teacher judgment is an important consideration in letting go of formal sit-down, paper-and-pencil testing for grading as also argued in earlier chapters. Not yet discussed at length, though, is the value of personalized learning which Tom Cook brings to life in this example.

To what extent should teachers' judgments be trusted for grading? Earlier chapters argue for the use of rubrics to strengthen these judgments, but realistically, rubrics are not fully developed in some cases. Often, they are just too time-consuming to create, but efforts should be made to do so. Interestingly, and perhaps as a model for K–12, most higher education courses now utilize rubrics for project and course grading, driven in large part by national accrediting agencies.

In his courses, Mr. Cook used rubrics that were developed in concert with his colleagues. When the "Participation in Government" course was rewritten, rubrics were developed by the entire team. In practice, modifications had to be made to adapt to changing requirements. In addition, Tom and his colleagues discussed these changes so that there was consistency within their building.

The extent of trust in teacher judgment lies in the degree of challenge that students (in this case, seniors) or their parents make about the validity of their grades. The "Participation in Government" course is required for graduation in the state of New York, making it high stakes. However, there were no grade challenges according to Tom, which is not surprising, given his experience, expertise, tenure as a highly qualified and admired teacher, and the research about the role of expertise in rendering judgments.

In U.S. courts of law or in arbitration hearings, expert witnesses or managers and superiors (if it's a hiring or firing case) called to testify are first asked to state their credentials to establish their level of expertise or credibility in the field. The Equal Employment Opportunity Commission (EEOC) has long held that professional expertise is an important consideration in hiring, firing, and promotion decisions.

For example, barring failure to follow stated procedures or exercising bias (which no doubt would be tested by the defendant's attorney), a principal's or superintendent's judgment concerning termination will stand up in court. Similarly, the same criteria hold true for hiring and promotion decisions. Thus, we should expect that same to be true for highly expert teachers grading student work.

The definition of *expert witness*, per the *Collins Dictionary of Law* is a

> person who is a specialist in a subject, often technical, who may present his/her expert opinion without having been a witness to any occurrence relating to the lawsuit or criminal case. It is an exception to the rule against giving an opinion in trial if the expert is qualified by evidence of his/her expertise, training and special knowledge. If the expertise is challenged, the attorney for the party calling the "expert" must make a showing of the necessary background through questions in court, and the trial judge has discretion to qualify the witness or rule he/she is not an expert, or is an expert on limited subjects.[2]

Unfortunately, despite all evidence to the contrary, many teachers and administrators are skittish about using *just* professional opinion for grading. Thus, in the United States we tend to rely much more on numeric grades as determined by sit-down, paper-and-pencil tests as described in earlier chapters—even though those test scores may very well be more unreliable and invalid than the teacher's expert judgment (see prior chapters).

But that is not the case everywhere. For example, New Zealand takes a very different viewpoint:

> Central to New Zealand National Standards is the concept of overall teacher judgements (OTJs). . . . To date, New Zealand has avoided the widely criticised national testing programmes introduced elsewhere, notably the No Child Left Behind policy introduced in the US in 2001. This is because New Zealand values the central role of formative assessment in improving learning and teaching, and the professionalism of its teachers.[3]

While there is some variability in the degree to which the New Zealand standards are implemented, overall success seems to be the case. That is not surprising, given the power and influence of expertise.

Mr. Cook's high school case study is also an excellent example of personalized learning—a popular and effective method of instruction today. Although most of the contemporary focus of personalized learning is on digital methodologies,[4] there exists a strong literature base supporting a personalized approach in all learning formats.

For example, in their comprehensive review, Buchem, Attwell, and Torres found strong support for the use of personal learning following certain rules and conventions. They state,

> Through the use of PLEs learners are seen as agents of their own process of change and designers of their own learning environment. The key roles of learners include taking ownership of own learning goals, processes and outcomes, taking responsibility for their own data and managing their online identity, taking leadership in learning settings and educational institutions and participating in social networks and communities.[5]

Chapter 9 by Barry Sheckley greatly expands on this topic. He shows the value of moving away from a direct or teacher-led instructional approach to one where students more actively engage in their own learning designs and setting goals. Tom Cook was well ahead of his time, as contemporary research clearly demonstrates the validity of his approach for maximal learning, let alone the challenging task of keeping seniors engaged.

TOM COOK'S "PARTICIPATION IN GOVERNMENT" COURSE

For almost four decades, Tom taught social studies in a central high school district on Long Island. During much of that time, he taught several sections of seniors each semester. In New York, seniors must pass the required "Participation in Government" and economics courses to graduate. As it happened, most seniors' names appeared on his class rosters at least once, as he taught several levels at the school.

Teaching seniors was a mixed blessing, he reports. They'd give their attention during the fall semester, but come spring, with a college acceptance letter in hand and warmer temperatures, many would begin to shut down. Still, they had to pass "PinG" ("Participation in Government") and "eco" (economics) to graduate, and it was his responsibility to keep them engaged until they succeeded.

One summer before the standardized testing craze, the district coordinator invited Tom to join others in rewriting the semester-long "Participation in Government" course. It would be unlike other social studies courses in that exams would be eliminated. Instead, each unit would involve an activity that would be both a learning experience and a means of evaluating students. The variety of activities would be a departure from the standard routine of a succession of units followed by unit exams.

For example, Tom notes that kids generically referred to one of the course activities as their how-to project. Formerly and more formally, it was called "Solving a Problem Related to Government." But his students liked calling it the how-to project, so he went with it. Seniors also had to attend a public meeting—school board, village, town, or county—and report on it. They interviewed public officials. They did presentations on landmark Supreme Court cases. Their "final exam" was an essay evaluating their thirty hours of community service. Again, all of this occurred over one semester for high school seniors in a required course that must be passed for graduation.

What follows are descriptions for some of those activities. There were no tests, just deep engagement by students—graded by teacher judgment based on standards set in the rubrics. In addition to the activities included here, there were many others, such as a presentation on a "problem" related to government, how to adopt a child, how to get a permit to build an addition on your house, how to acquire a passport, and how to legally disinter a body.

SAMPLE ACTIVITIES

The Scavenger Hunt

After completing an assignment investigating several dozen websites that provide information on federal, state, and local governments, students proceeded to the library. They received a handout with twenty-five questions related to government. For instance, "How many counties are in New York State?" "Who is your county legislator/county executive/state senator/state assemblyperson?" "What are the names of the incorporated cities in Nassau County?" "How many interstate highways/state parkways pass through Nassau and Suffolk Counties?" What is the oldest town on Long Island?" "In which town is the oldest cattle ranch in the U.S.?" "Who is the governor/ lieutenant governor/state comptroller?" "How many coast guard stations/ school districts/Indian reservations are on Long Island?" "When does the U.S. Supreme Court begin it session this year?"

Each question required three things of the students: the answer, the level of government, and two sources to substantiate the answer. Three versions were distributed. A fourth version was held in reserve for the few who did not submit their work before the graded papers were returned.

Answer sheets were collected from each class on the same day. Because each version was a different color, it was quick work to sort them. The next day, each class participated in grading one of the versions. No one was permitted to grade their own—two points for the answer, one point for the level of government, and one point for verification.

One question at a time, the answers were revealed on the overhead. It was an opportunity to reconsider some of the things discussed in class previously, and it was used to help them unravel the complexity of different levels of government in their lives. For example, just because a place is called Garden City does not mean it is an incorporated city; some Indian reservations are recognized by the state but not the federal government; living in a particular zip code does not mean you live in the incorporated village; your school district borders may include many hamlets, as well as other incorporated villages, and some may cross town or county lines.

Students were required to provide two separate sources for verification, but it was worth only one point. What if they provided only one source? At some point, Tom and his students reached a compromise. If the answer was correct and there was only one source, then they received full credit. However, if the answer was incorrect and there was only one source, then they lost credit for the answer and the source because, as they said, "they probably just copied it from someone else without double checking." Tom found that if they knew he was trying to treat them fairly, then they trusted the grading process.

Students could work together but were cautioned to verify everything they did, as so many websites contained outdated information. Tom's allies in this endeavor were the librarians, who wheeled out a cart containing local histories, atlases, almanacs, government directories, and the only hard copy that contained all the answers. It was a large binder that he had filled with newspaper articles, printouts, maps, and so on, organized by each level of government. Of course, given the go-ahead, almost all students raced to the computer stations, leaving the librarians chuckling about what they had left behind.

The Public Meeting

Students attended a public meeting—a school board, village board, town council, or county legislature. They had to acquire a copy of the agenda and write a report describing the conduct of the meeting from start to finish, including issues discussed, speakers, presentations made, and votes taken.

The Interview

Students interviewed an elected or an appointed official, such as the village mayor, their congressional representative, and individuals who worked for such service organizations as Ronald MacDonald House or the Red Cross. Some sources were interviewed every semester: Nassau County police officers and detectives, members of the school board, county and state legislators, the director of the public library, and volunteer firefighters. Often his students suggested new people to add to the mix: a coast guard officer, members of the military, an FBI agent, and even an elderly retired judge who first presided over a New York State school prayer case ultimately decided by the Supreme Court (*Engel v. Vitale*, 1962).

Students were not allowed to interview family members, although they could recommend them to their classmates. All prepared questions had to be submitted for approval to Tom prior to scheduling the interview because the "impertinence of youth" could produce questions that the subject might find offensive and thus bring the interview to an early conclusion, such as inquiring as to the average number of donuts consumed by the third precinct police officers! They were encouraged to ask follow-up questions to clarify previous responses. The write-up included an evaluation of how forthcoming the subject was during the interview.

The How-to Project

Students researched and did presentations on a "problem" related to government: how to adopt a child, how to get a building permit for an addition to your house, how to acquire a passport, how to legally disinter a body, how to become a citizen (a rather important topic in a district with more than 120 nationalities), how to incorporate a business in New York State, and so on. At an Eagle Scout induction ceremony, the town clerk told Tom how pleased she was that one of his students not only found out how to have stop signs installed but also proceeded to have them placed at a dangerous intersection near her home.

It is important to note that the problems presented were not of equal difficulty, so Tom added an element of chance and excitement to the selection process. The problems to be completed were numbered, and students drew the numbers out of a hat. If a student did not like the first selection, then they could draw one more time. Sounds like a Yankee swap at Christmastime!

Landmark Cases of the Supreme Court

Small teams researched cases, two originating on Long Island, and presented the issues involved, precedents, the vote, the majority, concurring and dissenting opinions, and relevant subsequent cases.

The Public Opinion Poll

Small teams of students selected a public issue—death penalty, immigration policy, and so on—and then constructed three questions to ask of their fellow seniors. Each team illustrated results in graphs or pie charts and led discussions in each class.

There were several other projects: "Public Issues," "We're Number One—or Not!" "Get to Know Your Representative," and "Special Interest Groups." Some were used every semester, and others were rotated or offered as extra credit. These projects were frequently revised and shared with colleagues who also taught the course. In addition to all these activities, there were guest speakers: assemblypersons, town councilmen, their county legislator, detectives, and judges, among others.

During the semester, Tom reports that there was indeed some testing. There were regular pop quizzes (ten minutes or so in length) on their local, state, and federal representatives. By the end of the semester, most students could identify their representatives better than their parents could. It was not uncommon for parents to relate how their sons or daughters had become more involved in political discussions at home.

FINAL EXAM PROXY

One-fifth of students' final grade was the final exam. Tom's district required that a semester course grade be calculated as follows: each quarter grade was doubled, thus the two quarters equaled 80 percent of the grade, and the semester or final exam was worth the remaining 20 percent.

In Tom's case, the "final exam" was based on thirty hours of community service completed during the semester. Tom distributed clearly defined guidelines as to what was acceptable and unacceptable service. For instance, on more than one occasion, Tom was asked by a student, "Can I get credit for community service for my Eagle Scout project?" or "Can I get credit for court-ordered community service?" In both instances, the answer was no; there would be no "double dipping." All students had to complete service within that semester in an activity solely for credit in the "Participation in Government" course.

Although presented with a long list of ideas, student-proposed alternatives were often allowed and quite interesting. They volunteered to work for hospitals, nursing homes, local firehouses, local sports programs, legislators' offices, political campaigns, the LI Children's Museum, and the Holocaust Memorial and Tolerance Center of Nassau County.

Some worked with special education students during the day. The experience of one tough customer, "Joe," was a pleasant revelation. After several weeks, the special ed teacher noted, "Whenever one of our kids is acting up, Joe looks at them and says 'Dude, that's not cool' and they stop what they were doing." "They look up to Joe," she continued. "They always give him a big greeting on the way to the cafeteria, and Joe always responds." It might have been the first time that Joe experienced being a positive role model for younger students. He did ask if he could work beyond the thirty hours because the "teacher says she needs me." Tom answered in the affirmative!

At times, Tom was told by students and their parents that the experience helped influence career choices. Many were asked to stay beyond the thirty hours, and every year, some were offered paid employment.

COURSE GRADING

As noted previously, the community service component was worth 20 percent of the final course grade. The community service grade was determined by assigning sixty points for thirty hours of service and forty points for the essay. That established their final exam grade, which was worth 20 percent of the course grade. The essay needed to address four areas: (1) preconceptions about the community service, (2) a detailed description of the typical responsibilities and daily activities during community service, (3) evaluation of the organization's service to the community, and (4) reflection on what the student got out of this service besides a passing grade. Each essay component was assigned ten points.

COURSE EPILOGUE: VOTER REGISTRATION

Near the end of the semester, each student was handed a voter registration form, which they completed, signed, sealed, addressed, and returned to Tom for delivery to the main office. Because the principal agreed that it was an appropriate culmination for the "Participation in Government" course, they were stamped and mailed.

The following are answers Mr. Cook provided to questions about his experiences teaching this course in a nontest environment. Given that this was a high-stakes course that seniors needed to pass for graduation, concern over completion of work and grading were important clarifications.

Question: Did any students or parents ever challenge the "nontest-based" quarterly, semester, or year-end grade?

Answer: Certainly parents would ask about their child's grades, but none asked that exams be used instead. On parent-teacher night, parents would receive copies of the course requirements, homework assignment sheets, projects, and so on. They were alerted to the old magazine assignment rack in the rear of the classroom, where extra copies of all handouts for each course were located. As a great patron of office supply stores, Tom acquired large quantities of colored copy paper. Projects were often color-coded, which made it easier for them to keep track of handouts. "I lost it," "I was absent when it was given out," and other assorted excuses were quickly undermined.

Question: Did students receive a rubric for each project? If so, who developed the rubrics?

Answer: Rubrics were distributed and reviewed with each project. Although originally developed by a committee of faculty earlier, Tom revised and improved rubrics over time and consulted with colleagues on the revisions.

Question: How did students get to their community project locations? Did transportation get in the way of student participation?

Answer: Attending a public meeting would require transportation. Students would travel with friends who were licensed drivers or with their parents. Tom indicated that he liked the second option. Parents would not only have a better understanding of what was required of their children but also could attend a school board or village board meeting, perhaps for the first time.

Rarely was it an impossibility to attend; even the parents of one child confined to a wheelchair transported her to a meeting, although she could not do community service. Nevertheless, Tom had no problem working with parents and students who faced imposing difficulties. That's why he employed alternate activities. Despite having most of the semester to complete the required hours for community service, on rare occasions this was not possible.

One year, a young man and a young lady lacked the time altogether. Their parents confirmed that, between sports, after-school jobs, and a tight schedule during the day, they couldn't perform community service outside of school or during the school day. Tom assigned them a public issues project instead.

Question: How well did students perform in this class, generally speaking?

Answer: In his district, mid–marking period progress reports were distributed, which provided an opportunity to notify parents that a child was "Not meeting course requirements," "Frequently absent," or "Cuts class." Of course, no teacher worth one's salt waits until those reports. Never spring a surprise on a parent if an earlier phone call can correct the problem.

Without exaggeration, it was exceedingly rare for a senior to fail these courses. Tom tried to find multiple ways to acknowledge their good efforts. They received a homework grade each marking period that was equal to a full-period exam. At least five pop quizzes were given each marking period. The lowest grade was dropped because everyone has a bad day, especially on Mondays. They were averaged as a test grade. They received a class participation grade each marking period. The most likely reason for a student to fail was that he or she ran afoul of the district's attendance policy. That made it difficult for him to launch an appeal on their behalf.

Question: How long a time period (in days or weeks) would each of these activities take to complete?

Answer:

The Scavenger Hunt: Two or three research days in the library. The answer sheet was submitted shortly thereafter.

The Public Meeting: One day in class prepping them and checking official websites for the dates of the meetings, which were projected from the Proxima. Generally, two to three weeks.

The Interview: Generally, two to three weeks. Tom viewed and approved questions before and after school or during free periods. Sometimes adjustments were made because the mayor, county legislator, and so on had scheduling difficulties. If the same person was being interviewed by teams in more than one class, they tried to coordinate a common appointment.

The How-to Project: One day to prep and select topics by lottery. Two weeks to complete before class presentations were to begin. Depending on class size, four to five days of presentations.

Landmark Cases of the Supreme Court: Two to three days spent researching in the library and two to three days doing presentations in class.

The Public Opinion Poll: About one day in class to help them craft appropriate questions and one day to poll fellow students in their class. (Early on, there was an incident in one of the other buildings in which seniors went out into the neighborhood and asked questions about drug use. Not good! In addition, one former chair of Tom's was concerned when seniors in the senior cafeteria asked juniors and sophomores questions about birth control and condoms. So, he limited the sample polled to each class. When the results of all three classes were added together, it still gave a good picture of what seniors thought about the issues.)

Question: Instead of these activities, approximately how many unit tests might they have had if it was taught traditionally? Would each of the unit tests take a normal-length period to complete?
Answer: There would have been several tests each marking period, each one period long.

Question: Quizzes were still used. Approximately how often (once a week, more, less)? And how much class time would they typically take to complete?
Answer: Once a week. Ten questions on a transparency on the overhead projector. Ten minutes. Within that ten minutes, once they signaled completion, they exchanged papers, and the quizzes were quickly graded.

Question: Regarding the final exam, what did it replace had you taught this material traditionally? And how much class time (including any prep needed) would all that have taken up?
Answer: Generally, a final exam would involve one day for multiple choice and one day for an essay.

SUMMARY

Had Tom taught this semester-long course in a more traditional format, he would have administered two to three major tests per marking period or quarter. Each test would have taken up a full period in length; thus, by not utilizing tests for grading, he saved five to six periods per full semester that were reclaimed for instruction, discussion, and student engagement. This time savings exceeds assumptions made in earlier chapters about the amount of time that could be reclaimed for instruction by limiting the traditional use of tests in the classroom.

More importantly, by using projects and personalizing these experiences, students were engaged in ways that they might not otherwise be normally. And anyone who has taught seniors will recognize that this is a gross understatement! Instead of just going through the motions to pass a required course in government, this content was brought alive in ways that fully engaged seniors on the brink of graduation and prone to serious senioritis.

Finally, grading was completed in a thorough and in-depth manner, not through traditional tests resulting in numeric grades, rather through projects that are self-evidently completed successfully or not. As shown by the fact that neither parents nor students challenged grades in this high-stakes course needed for graduation, it makes the case for a different approach to traditional testing used for grading.

One last way to look at this case study is from a cost-efficiency perspective. Tom Cook and his colleagues are highly trained, experienced experts, commanding high education salaries. Not discussed in this chapter is the partner social studies course also required for seniors to graduate—economics—for which Tom and his colleagues used much the same practices. Thus, we can safely say that he effectively added between ten and twelve instructional days to the year. Based on a 180-day school year, Tom has effectively increased that by about 6 percent or more. Imagine what that would cost the school district to implement across the board!

There was no need for the traditional midterm or final exam that would take up four days of the high school yearly calendar. As discussed in earlier chapters, there are benefits to exposing kids to these types of high-stakes testing environments, but it is not necessary for every subject, every term, every year.

Think of the possibilities in many other courses if similar instructional and grading procedures were followed in Tom's school or yours. In science, research projects and lab demonstrations could replace sit-down tests. English class essays of every type would be much more engaging than traditional tests. Mathematics might be more difficult to pull off, but showing the application of theorems to such problems as how to use calculus or vector mathematics to plan a trajectory to Mars would be an interesting diversion. The arts are self-explanatory.

While it will not be possible to transform every course in departmentalized middle and high schools as Tom did with this "Participation in Government" course, surely many teachers could replace some of their traditional tests with performance-based expositions for grading. Previous chapters advocate for a 25 percent reduction in traditional testing to reclaim that time for instruction. That seems like a very achievable goal, considering the guidance Tom Cook and his colleagues demonstrate in this case study.

NOTES

1. Thomas Cook can be contacted at thmcook6@aol.com.

2. "Expert witness." *The Free Dictionary by Farlex.* 2017. http://legal-diction-ary.thefreedictionary.com/Expert+witnesses.

3. Poskitt, Jenny, and Kerry Mitchell. "New Zealand teachers' overall teacher judgements (OTJs): Equivocal or unequivocal?" *Assessment Matters* 4 (2012): 53.

4. "Taking stock of personalized learning." *Education Week.* October 20, 2014. http://www.edweek.org/ew/collections/personalized-learning-special-report-2014/index.html?intc=highsearch.

5. Buchem, Ilona, Graham Attwell, and Ricardo Torres. "Understanding personal learning environments: Literature review and synthesis through the activity theory lens." *Proceedings of the PLE Conference, Southampton, UK* (July 10–12, 2011): 28.

Chapter Eight

The Pathway to a Positive Culture

Richard Ayers

Is it reasonable to expect that all public schools be held to the same standards, regardless of sociological and economic stature? Are schools' test scores the single determinate of the value of a school?

Educational leaders know that adapting to the call for greater accountability in school policy is important. But nearly all find this unnerving, as it forces them to confront strategies to transform the organization in a way that is potentially beyond their control. Motivating an established culture is difficult, say nothing about setting a direction that is speculative. This speaks to the dilemma facing many educational leaders: Is the prevailing emphasis on proficiency-based instruction measured by a progression of achievement scores an accurate reflection of the quality of the school and its ability to adapt to future needs?

The irony is that schools are less commonly recognized within their communities for the image they project in terms of a cohesive and collaborative learning environment that reflects the values of the community. Rather, they are much more likely to be judged by the traditional profile of test scores, which is a policy distractor in a much larger spectrum of cultural attributes that speaks to the "true value" of schools. In general, this relates to the culture of schools that aims to be value driven, purposeful in articulating priorities, and balanced in dependence on a wide range of factors to define their relevance.

Schools that measure success solely on the range of standardized assessments of student achievement are likely missing the far greater value of a constructive, balanced culture for learning. An interesting observation is that schools and school district's that give greater attention to the culture and provide a well-thought-out approach to the testing program are more likely to score higher on tests. In other words, is the worth of a school or district measured by their test scores, without consideration for the demographics or sociological challenges within their schools?

Several factors have traditionally influenced public opinion on the *value* of schools. These range from the preparation of graduates for higher education careers to the satisfaction of families with their children's education. Additional factors include options students have in extracurricular activities, along with such factors as dropout and graduation rates. More specifically, parents tend to be concerned with factors like grades for class work, SAT or ACT scores, and college acceptance rates.

The declining stature of our nation's educational reputation, a result of international test scores, along with an increasing disparity in the opportunities for economically disadvantaged students, has prompted an increase in federal and state mandates over the last several decades. NCLB and now ESSA require continued testing of students in select grades and subject matter, as well as the initiation of the Common Core curriculum. Continued rankings, predominantly based on these test scores, have raised public consciousness of the perceived quality of their schools, even if there is little basis for making such determinations. Such policies have significantly affected school culture.

The cumulative effect of these changes places schools and their leaders in a position to respond to three factors that influence the success of their organization: (1) federal mandates on Common Core and test scores, (2) statewide comparisons of their school's educational profile (largely made up of test scores), and (3) the community's interpretation of the relative quality of their schools.

These factors have significant impact on the community's perception of the quality of their schools, which in turn influence internal operations and priorities. Public perception places schools, their officials, and their elected board members in a position of defending the quality of the organization; the competency of the administration, faculty, and staff; and the value of a community's investment in their schools.

The inference is that the culture of schools must be transformed to meet the wide array of expectations beyond just improving achievement scores. This is often referred to as the twenty-first-century school, suggesting that schools must be forward-thinking with a mind-set for innovation, collaboration, and the collective will to strategically embrace change.

THE ELEMENTS OF CULTURE

Culture is defined as the "manifestations of human intellectual achievement regarded collectively."[1] This infers a school culture that recognizes the importance of collaboration in creating an environment that is centered on a core set of values and is coherent in the application of primary goals to advance student learning and personal growth. Fullan and Quinn bring attention to the importance of "consistency of purpose, policy and practice in schools and school districts to make good on the promise of public education."[2] They present a framework that is based on four primary factors that influence the coherence of a school culture: (1) focused direction, (2) goals that impact, (3) clarity of strategy, and (4) change leadership.[3]

Without going into detail of the four elements, the Fullan and Quinn framework is representative of the depth of purposeful organizational development schools must embrace to promote learning at a higher level. Peter Senge states, "Organizations work the way they work because of the ways that people think and interact."[4] This is the case in point required for schools to change their culture to a new norm that is more broadly visible and accountable to their communities.

The subtler element of culture is the motivation to transform an organizational setting that is often traditional in mind-set and reluctant to adapt to more sophisticated methodologies. In many cases, it is more related to the acceptance of why the traditional framework must change than what must be done to significantly improve the organization. Clarity in the why is the essential foundation for motivating people within an organization.

A *Harvard Business Review* article, "How Company Culture Shapes Employee Motivation," states that three fundamental questions can help transform an organizational culture: (1) How does the culture drive performance? (2) What is culture worth? and (3) What processes in an organization affect culture?[5] The authors note that, following an analysis of 50 major companies and more than 20,000 workers and reviewing academic research in a range of disciplines, they came to one conclusion: *Why we work determines how well we work.* The article goes on to cite the research of Edward Deci and Richard Ryan from the University of Rochester, who distinguished the six main reasons people work. The first three are considered good motives:

1. **Play** is when you are motivated by the work itself. You work because you enjoy it. . . .
2. **Purpose** is when the direct outcome of the work fits your identity. You work because you value the work's impact. . . .
3. **Potential** is when the outcome of the work benefits your identity. . . . [T]he work enhances your potential.[6]

The authors note that, when these motives are directly connected to the work itself, people are better motivated. These are direct motives. The following indirect motives, however, tend to reduce performance:

1. **Emotional pressure** is when you work because some external force threatens your identity. . . . This motive is completely separate from the work itself. . . .
2. **Economic pressure** is when an external force makes you work. You work to gain a reward or avoid a punishment. . . .
3. **[I]nertia** is when the motive is so far removed from the work and your identity that you can't identify why you're working.[7]

Translating these insights into practice is no easy task. An initiative that is exceedingly difficult, absent the will and motivation within the organization to improve, is likely to fail. Educational organizations that embrace these concepts on motivation would be well served to establish a means of engaging individuals and teams in informal assessments of their views regarding the positive influences of play, purpose, and potential.

Research on effective organizational culture specific to schools implies that school culture drives performance. Schools that achieve coherence within the organizational culture are much more likely to adapt to the mandated testing regimen than the testing regimen dictating the priorities of the organization. Thus, in the best of worlds, culture adapts to testing along with the multitude of other external sanctions placed on schools.

The reality is that schools with sufficient resources and advantaged demographics are more likely to achieve a higher degree of balance within the school culture necessary to create and sustain a high profile on standardized tests. However, settings with limited resources and high concentrations of disadvantaged populations are likely to have marginal performances on tests and a greater challenge in sustaining a cohesive culture, as reinforced in chapter 10.

Given the socioeconomic disparity of communities and consequently their schools, the expectation that *all* schools reach proficiency within the same time frame is unrealistic and clearly discouraging. As to be expected, this has a significant impact on the culture of schools that are confronted with an often-insurmountable goal. The one-size-fits-all expectation, coupled with expanded use of testing, seriously undermines efforts to create and sustain a cohesive and forward-thinking school culture. If there was a formula to calculate gains in student achievement rather than using status scores, growth in achievement would be the major focus enabling the development of a positive culture.

STRATEGY

Strategy is how an organization goes from what it is to what it aims to be. It is a matter of adapting or directing current actions to desired goals in a planned manner. Marshall Ganz states that development of effective strategy is more likely to occur under conditions in which strategists are highly motivated, enjoy access to diverse sources of salient knowledge, and employ deliberate practices committed to learning in what he calls *strategic capacity*.[8] As Ganz states,

> Motivation influences creative output because it affects the focus one brings to one's work, the ability to concentrate for extended periods of time, persistence, willingness to take risks, and ability to sustain high energy. Motivated individuals are more likely to do the work to acquire needed knowledge and skills. . . . A second element of creativity is possession of skills, mastery of which is requisite for developing novel applications. . . . Access to a diversity of salient knowledge not only offers multiple routines from which to choose, but also contributes to the "mindfulness" that multiple solutions are possible.[9]

SYSTEM LEADERSHIP

Public school organizations are, in many respects, outdated and restrained by the limitations inherent to the schooling traditions that reach far back in history. However, there are many examples of school cultures that have created and sustained a high-quality education to an increasingly diverse student population. In such cases, the common denominator is sound, informed, and often-courageous leadership.

Margaret Wheatley, applying the new science to leadership theory, proposes that the way to truly lead organizations is to accept that change is the only predictable reality; anyone can be a leader, and when any individual acts, he or she will find like-minded others that ultimately form a grassroots leadership force capable of sustainable change in a constantly changing and chaotic world. These leaders have a new role in fostering the culture and environment of the organization itself to ensure that solutions can emerge safely, authentically, and effectively. This means that new leaders must embrace their own vulnerability and willingly accept their role to serve in this type of environment.[10]

Fullan and Quinn, in their book *Coherence: The Right Drivers in Action for Schools, Districts, and Systems*, state that local leaders have to play their part in establishing internal accountability systems and relating to the external accountability system by focusing direction, cultivating collaborative cultures, and deepening learning.[11] With this in mind, the consensus on role of the organizational leader appears to surround two basic factors: cultivating integrity within the organization and ensuring prominent results.

Reaching this level of proficiency requires a clear and commanding sense of purpose, a forward-thinking design for achieving improvement, an articulate plan for implementation of the change process, and a means of engaging all stakeholders in the change process. The following is an example of the elements within each of these key factors in the transformation process.

Clarity in Purpose

- Statement of a collectively cultivated vision that encompasses a capability and capacity to succeed.
- Statement of the primary opportunities to realize the vision as well as the challenges.
- Statement of the value of reaching the desired outcomes for the educational enterprise.
- Statement of the rewards for all who are committed to this purpose, students, and the parents and community who made the achievements possible.
- Chronology of the research on change, innovation, and transformation of organizational cultures.
- Willingness to broaden the circle of participants who support the mission and be actively engaged in sustaining the intended purpose.

Integrity in the Architecture of the Change Process

- Creation of a blueprint for change that illustrates the requirements essential to meet desired results.
- Creation of the function or essential strategies to meet the desired outcomes.
- Establishment of the methodologies for development and implementation of the elements of the strategies.
- Demonstration of the inclusive nature of the developmental process as well as the parameters for decision making in design, development, and construction of the strategic culture.
- Creation of the crucial path for meeting desired outcomes in a logical time frame and illustrating the basic components crucial for full implementation.
- Reinforcement of the challenges, opportunities, and rewards of contributing to the developmental process.
- Establishment of a communication plan that ensures regular updates to all constituents of the transformation process and that reinforces the purpose, progress, and observations at each stage of the process.

Engagement in the Construction of the Transformation of the Organizational Culture

- Establishment of a collaborative and inclusive team to design steps for development.
- Development of a model for program effectiveness to use as a template for implementation.
- Ensuring cost-effectiveness within available resources.
- Ensuring that piloting of the process is undertaken in the school and is monitored and evaluated by the design and implementation teams.
- Refinement of the model as appropriate and preparation for full implementation.
- Development of a process for monitoring, documenting impact (data), and modification of design and implementation process, and so on.
- Creation of a well-crafted and widely distributed announcement of the culture and its benefits to primarily students, as well as stakeholders in the schools and community.

These core elements of the change process serve as an example of the scope of factors that contribute to the necessary planning by leaders, whether superintendent or principal, to lead the transformation process.

ORGANIZATIONAL FITNESS

There are many aspects of organizational culture in the business world that have relevancy to the culture of schools. This section illustrates those insights about culture that translate to education.

Daniel Kahneman, professor emeritus of psychology at Princeton University, and his colleagues wrote about the factor he referred to as "noise" in organizations that expect consistency from their employees. By noise, he refers to such irrelevant factors as the weather and the last case seen (or, in the case of schools, the latest incident on the playground or the score of the latest game). He continues with the notion that errors in judgment are most likely social bias, like stereotyping of minorities, or cognitive bias, such as overconfidence and unfounded optimism. Overcoming noise and bias in an organization must be a priority for the system leader, who approaches the transformation of a culture to a more focused and analytical reasoning model.[12]

The advancement or transformation of a school culture requires attention to motivational factors as well as a strategic approach to establishing consistency in decision making, leadership roles, and instructional practices. The "Elevation of Thought" model in figure 8.1 incorporates elements of Kahneman and colleauges' recommended strategies that are akin to the philosopher Soren Kierkegaard's portrait on a "leap of faith."[13] The model represents the transitions of thought and reason for an organization that alters the nature of their culture from half-truths to one that cultivates a higher order of thinking and establishes a climate where innovation, creativity, and high standards for performance are expected and rewarded.

Given the intense effort required to change a school's culture, how may a superintendent or building leader best approach this challenge? The foremost factor is the will or determination to construct an environment where employees are committed to their work because they believe in the mission and are supported through effective channels of communication in a comfortable, supportive working environment. The leader must be cognizant of the factors that commonly lead to job dissatisfaction, such as uncomfortable working conditions and disconnected relationships with supervisors.

Noise/Aesthetics	Conceptual Reasoning	Enlightenment/Salient Knowledge
Incidental occurrences Aesthetics-weather, style Small talk	Critical thinking/problem solving Ideas Collaborative efforts Innovation in practice	Tangible results Inspirational Achievements Inspiring, productive culture

Figure 8.1. Elevation of thought. Kahneman, Daniel, Andrew M. Rosenfield, Linnea Gandhi, and Tom Blaser. "Noise: How to overcome the high, hidden cost of inconsistent decision making." *Harvard Business Review* **94, no. 10 (October 2016).**

Leaders must be systemic in transforming a school or district's culture. As Kahneman and colleagues state, "Studies have shown that while humans can provide input, algorithms do better in the role of final decision makers."[14] With this in mind, the leader should create a design or model in her own mind for the transformation process, which others might call a theory of action. The value of the leader giving attention to this is twofold: First, they project what they believe to be an obtainable outcome in each time frame because of the effort required, and second, they project anticipated major challenges and opportunities in reaching the desired outcome.[15]

PATHWAY TO A POSITIVE CULTURE

Each of the elements of this transformation process requires an articulate and inclusive framework that reflects the expressed vision and core values of the organization. Figures 8.2, 8.3, and 8.4 on clarity of purpose, architectural integrity, and developmental or construction plan present in more detail the crucial elements expressed earlier of the transformation process.

As to be expected, the suggested strategies in these figures are, at times, subject to marginal success throughout the organizational transformation process. We can expect sometimes-unsettling cultural change in schools that all organizations go through in the transformation process. The leader's dilemma in orchestrating cultural transformation is to sustain momentum. Unfortunately, this can be difficult due to leadership changes often driven by shifting politics of governing boards, increasing state and federal regulations, and funding problems. A strategy to consider is for the leader to deliberately disperse decision-making authority within the organization. If the ownership

Objective	Intended Results	Strategy
Solidify a Vision	United identity with Vision and implications for individual, organization, community	Engagement of stakeholders in construct of Vision statement
Translate Vision to opportunities as well as challenges to actualize	Clarity and exposure to opportunities and challenges	Establish process for defining opportunities and challenges by Steering Task Force and publication of findings
Establish Core Values for meeting tenants of Vision Statement	Conscious attention to Core Values in all aspects of school or district culture	Steering Task Force initiates process for establishing Core Values, publication. district/school administration design process for adaptation to culture
Insure united recognition of the recognition of the value for individuals and organization in reaching vision and adhering to core values	Understanding of the importance of reaching vision, adoption of core values and solidifying motivation to achieve	District/building administration establish process for dialogue, engagement in staff in recognizing relevance and cultivating common ambition to achieve results
Provide framework for Process in reaching Vision as profiled in literature, specific examples in educational settings	Understanding the magnitude of the process, effort and reliance of individual commitment to achieve desired results	District/building administrative teams create transparent and inclusive process for conducting research, publication and presentation

Figure 8.2.   Clarity of purpose.

is shared and responsibility for decision making strategically dispersed, then sustainability of the change process is more likely to succeed.

THE LEADER'S PERSPECTIVE

The telos of organizational leadership centers on a clear and focused sense of purpose. Conger and Kanungo define *purpose* as the ability of an individual to influence a group toward the achievement of goals. Simply said, care for people and care for results. [16]

The Superintendent: Validation of Vision and Values

As previously mentioned, the superintendent's role in the development of the district's vision and core values is a top priority. The process gives a sense of the potential of the district in reaching a higher level of sustainability and, in turn, results. In a sense, the superintendent serves as the district's historian.

Objective	Intended Results	Strategy
Establish blueprint/model for change process	Well-crafted pathway to reach intended results	Establish Design Task Force to create the Design/Model for reaching desired results, in detail
Define specific strategies for transforming the school/district culture	Adoption of the design/model that defines the intricacies of commitment to the change process	Design Task force introduces design options in details inclusive of suggested strategies for implementation, validation and revision in time
Acquaintance with methodologies and necessary commitment in design process	Understanding of the intricacies of the methodologies and commitments to the developmental process	Design Task force and district/building administration create the index of methodologies, opportunities for input, and process for unfolding the design/model for cultural transformation
Clarity in process and implications for decision making in the implementation process	Transparency in the development process and willing engagement and contribution to the process	Establish process for communication and engagement in the design process to include recognition of pilot sites
Establish the Critical Path for the implementation process that is attentive to timeline, measures of validation and completion of process	Transparency in process and understanding of timeline, implications and increments of change process	Design Team in concert with district/building administrative team construct critical Path document and plan for recognizing increments of progress and necessary adaptations to document and process
Establish plan for progress reports and necessary revisions to design	Regular communications to stakeholders on progress, revisions and map of progress toward major objectives	Design Team establishes process and responsibilities for Communications and necessity for revision or modification to elements of the project design

Figure 8.3. Architectural integrity.

The extent to which the district can be transformed in a realistic time frame is supported by a clear sense of the cultural norms of the past.

The district's leadership group should follow the same pattern as that envisioned for the transformation of the district's culture; that is, to reaffirm the district's vision and core values and align the group's efforts around three to five primary district goals. The superintendent's responsibility is to first determine the composition of the leadership group or team (within her or his degree to influence that team), then establish criteria for the team's responsibilities, and initiate a process to establish norms for the team's conduct and decision making. Equally important is the structure for applying the decisions of the team at each level of the organization, as well as the format for communication of their decisions.

The superintendent's role is to ensure that the team's efforts are directly tied to the district's priorities (goals) and that the norms are upheld in the team's efforts. Responsibilities within the team should be dispersed for establishing an agenda, recording minutes, and sharing implications and expec-

Objective	Intended results	Strategy
Establish an inclusive Construction Oversight Team	A carefully administered process for implementation of the plan for transformation of the school/district culture	Create a template for oversight of process for implementation and select representatives from stakeholder group for representation
Establish template for the Construction process that meets components of the design/model and critical path documents	A comprehensive plan and process for Construction	Oversight Team initiates construction process and oversees the strategies. District/school administrative teams determine role administration will take in engaging staff in process
Implement Construction Plan within projected budget, timeframe and intended profile for results	Fully transparent and engaging process in implementation of validated plan for implementation of transformation of the school/district culture	Oversight Team closely monitor the construction process, present progress reports in timely manner with notation of progress in reaching intended goal/outcome
Recognize increments of progress in meeting objectives of the Transformation Plan and recognize notable achievements	Recognize resultant advancements in the culture of the district/school and insure that elements of transformation are solidified and identified in terms of advancement in performance, student achievement	Insure progress in Construction of renewed culture consistent with published desired outcomes Recognition of achievements, expanse of participation and influence upon students, family, community, faculty and staff, etc.

Figure 8.4. Developmental or construction plan.

tations. This includes ensuring that agenda items are categorized in relationship to primary goals, with a clear statement of purpose and intended results.

The superintendent is the key element in connecting the school district to the greater community. Traditionally, superintendents have a predictable role in ensuring that community representation in their school district is consistent with the crucial elements of governance; policy development; and, to some extent, engagement in their schools.

With the continued emphasis still on ranking school and district test scores, districts are often placed in a position of being defensive about the value of the educational program. As such, the superintendent must accept the task of informing and engaging the greater community about their schools. Suggested strategies include

1. Engaging the governing board (school board or board of directors) in a process of communicating with constituents on the priorities and strategic improvement efforts of their schools.

2. Developing a learning plan, like the traditional marketing plan for organizations that speaks to the vision, core values, and goals of the district in understandable language.
3. Engaging community members in open forums on educational challenges and opportunities in the twenty-first century.
4. Publishing guides for parents and community members on how they may be involved in their schools.
5. Inviting parents and community members to be involved directly in the learning process in schools, particularly in project-based learning initiatives.
6. Inviting parents and community members to participate through district-centered social media opportunities.
7. Involving district administrators and teachers in community-based service groups.
8. Developing partnerships with community-based organizations and businesses in promotion of cooperative programs for students, staff, and administrators.
9. Publishing an annual report card on the district's accomplishments toward meeting goals and a catalogue of achievements, as well as notation of areas where further emphasis must be placed in the year ahead.
10. Publishing a monthly message that follows a theme, such as "A School within a Community, A Community within a School," where brief vignettes of notable aspects of the district's culture for learning are highlighted.

The Principal: Validation of Vision and Values

In many respects, the principal's role mirrors that of the superintendent. The principal's primary task is to interpret what is applicable in expression and action in the individual school setting. For instance, while the district goals are a primary factor in the framework of the school culture, they should be implemented with the input of faculty and staff on the best approach to teaching and learning in the school. This could be in the form of specific improvement objectives for the instructional program or a refined statement of purpose and intended results that are specific to the school. This is as important as the in-depth statement of strategies and methodologies that are used to improve the school culture and its programs.

An article in *Education Week* by Denisa Superville speaks to these new dimensions in leadership training for principals. She notes, "As organizational leaders, principals need to have the same kinds of skill sets that effective managers in other professions possess: the ability to create a compelling vision, lead high performing teams, think like problem solvers, and execute on plans."[17] As with the superintendent, this illustrates the necessity of principals to become knowledgeable about organizational improvement culture.

The characteristic of a thriving, student-focused community of learners should be on display in schools. The strength of a school's culture takes on the characteristics of a caring community that embraces the value of their children's educational experiences. Similar in the fashion of the superintendent, the principal must inform and engage the external community in the "life" of their schools. Suggested strategies include:

1. Engaging the teachers and staff in efforts to communicate the relevance of the educational programs and practices to parents and the community at large.
2. Ensuring that statements of beliefs and purpose are visible throughout the school and clearly stated in publications and on social media.
3. Promoting the achievements of the school on a regular basis on billboards or electronic information postings, such as "We are proud that 85 percent of our students were proficient in math this year; our goal is 100 percent."
4. Establishing a parent and community advisory committee to involve parents and community members in their school. This could conclude with a yearly celebration of parent and community involvement in their schools where local officials, business leaders, and so on are invited and recognized for their support and assistance to student learning and achievement.
5. Promoting the value of personal contact with parents by teachers committing to contact each parent with a personal phone call to discuss with them their child's progress and contribution to the classroom or school. Although this is more common at the elementary and middle school levels, the value of personal calls or notes to students and parents at the high school level is equally as significant.
6. Constructing a profile of the school that includes all the elements of the culture, such as vision and core values, information on scope of programs, and learning opportunities, as well as graphics that display

comparison of achievement scores to state average, among other things. This is a marketing plan for a school that speaks to the value of the educational process and the benefit served to all who are a part of the school community.

7. As recommended for the superintendent, publishing a yearly report card and monthly newsletter that is attentive to the value of the educational experience within the school.

The principalship is a demanding yet most rewarding position. The reward is in seeing firsthand the impact that a cohesive and coherent culture has on the advancements in achievement and personal development of students.

SUMMARY

In closing, this chapter recognizes the importance of the intricacies of the school culture. Thus, there is a relationship of school culture with the success of the educational programs within a school. The strength and relevancy of the culture is dependent on four key factors: a clear sense of purpose, a well-thought-out and cohesive strategy to achieve results, a collective will or motivation to succeed, and an informed and collaborative decision-making process. Leaders who can build this kind of culture will have much more success in achieving all their improvement goals.

The focus of this book is on how to recapture crucial instructional time from wasted or unnecessary testing practices, particularly from nonmandated testing. It is pointed out in earlier chapters that just recapturing time is insufficient for success. Real improvement is based on what is done with that time. The types of instructional improvements advocated throughout this book, but particularly in the next chapter by Barry Sheckley, are very difficult to achieve without a school culture that promotes and welcomes change and innovation. Thus, the approaches to improving culture argued here are important in making those changes to the learning continuum, such as the mandated testing paradigm.

NOTES

1. "Culture." *English Oxford Living Dictionaries.* 2017. https://en.oxforddictionaries.com/definition/culture.

2. Fullan, Michael, and Joanne Quinn. *Coherence: The right drivers in action for schools, districts, and systems.* Thousand Oaks, CA: Corwin, 2016.

3. Ibid.

4. O'Neill, John. "On schools as learning organizations: A conversation with Peter Senge." *Educational Leadership* 52, no. 7 (April 1995): 20–23.

5. McGregor, Lindsay, and Neel Doshi. "How company culture shapes employee motivation." *Harvard Business Review*. November 25, 2015. https://hbr.org/2015/11/how-company-culture-shapes-employee-motivation.

6. Ibid.

7. Ibid.

8. Ganz, Marshall. "Leading change: Leadership, organization, and social movements." In *Handbook of leadership theory and practice: A Harvard Business School centennial colloquium on advancing leadership*, edited by Nitin Nohria and Rakesh Khurana, pp. 527–68. Boston: Harvard Business Press, 2010.

9. Ibid.

10. Madsen, Susan R., and Scott C. Hammond. "'Where have all the leaders gone?' An interview with Margaret J. Wheatley on life-affirming leadership." *Journal of Management Inquiry* 14, no. 1 (March 2005): 71–77.

11. Fullan and Quinn, *Coherence*.

12. Kahneman, Daniel, Andrew M. Rosenfield, Linnea Gandhi, and Tom Blaser. "Noise: How to overcome the high, hidden cost of inconsistent decision making." *Harvard Business Review* (October 2016).

13. Solomon, Robert C., and Kathleen M. Higgins. *A Short History of Philosophy*. New York: Oxford University Press, 1996.

14. Kahneman et al., "Noise."

15. Ibid.

16. Conger, Jay A., and Rabindra N. Kanungo. "Toward a behavioral theory of charismatic leadership in organizational settings." *Academy of Management Review* 12, no. 4 (October 1987): 637–47.

17. Superville, Denisa R. "Leaders go to school to learn management savvy." *Education Week*. November 4, 2015.

Chapter Nine

What to Do with Reclaimed Instructional Time

Barry Sheckley

Teachers and administrators who follow the suggestions outlined in prior chapters to reduce the amount of class time devoted to testing may wonder, "Now what?" Of course, the extra time could be used to double down on the curriculum and devote more time to teach each instructional unit. There is another very viable option: Help students improve their use of self-regulated learning (SRL) strategies to advance their own learning. This suggestion is aligned with a wide body of research on the strong relationship between students' use of SRL strategies and gains in achievement.[1]

When students self-regulate their learning, they typically engage in a three-phase, ever-repeating cycle in which they focus their thoughts, behaviors, and reflections on attaining specific learning goals.[2] In the first phase of the cycle, learners typically clarify their expectations, set goals, and outline plans. During the second phase, they employ strategies that are specific to the task, engage in self-talk to monitor their progress, and seek help as appropriate. In the third phase, they reflect on their work, identify factors that affected their performance, and develop adaptive responses that inform their plans and expectations for their next cycle of learning.

A broad array of research confirms that enhancing students' ability to use SRL strategies has a robust relationship with gains in academic achievement. In a meta-analysis based on 263 effect sizes from 48 studies, Dignath, Buettner, and Langfeldt report that training students to use SRL strategies resulted in about a 20 percent improvement in academic performance.[3] In another meta-analysis of 63 different studies, Hattie found that students' use of SRL strategies, such as planning how to approach a learning task, evaluating progress, and monitoring comprehension, was related to a 23 percent improvement in achievement.[4] These gains in achievement are almost double the gains achieved, on average, by educational interventions.

In one example, Nagle, Sheckley, and Allen explore ways to help eighth-grade science students in an urban school use SRL strategies to enhance their learning.[5] Two classes were randomly assigned to an intervention in which students used SRL strategies, and two classes were assigned to a more traditional instruction condition (TRAD). Each condition included classes designated by the district as "accelerated" (ACCL; higher-performing) and "academic" (ACAD; lower-performing).

The intervention followed a three-phase format used in prior research.[6] In phase 1, the teacher conducted mini-lessons for students in both conditions. In the TRAD condition, he emphasized good study habits (e.g., taking notes). In the SRL condition, he outlined the cognitive SRL strategies (e.g., elaboration skills) and metacognitive SRL strategies (e.g., self-evaluation skills) that have the strongest relationships with improvements in students' achievement.[7] Students in both conditions discussed ways to incorporate into their work the ideas covered in the respective mini-lessons.

In phase 2, the teacher devoted equal amounts of time to students in both conditions during discussions every other week that focused on entries in their notebooks. In initial discussions with TRAD students, the teacher helped them write in their notebooks a goal for the unit and ways they could achieve this goal. In subsequent discussions, he discussed their notebook entries, checked their grades, and answered their questions about topics covered in the course. In initial discussions with SRL students, the teacher helped them outline in their notebooks two to three curricular goals (e.g., learn Newton's laws of motion), two to three goals on becoming a better learner (e.g., improve my self-monitoring skills), and two to three specific SRL strategies they would use to achieve these goals (e.g., using problem-solving skills effectively). In subsequent discussions, he helped them sharpen their causal attributions by providing feedback in a way that helped them adjust their use of SRL strategies on their next learning task.[8]

In phase 3, students in both groups independently and continually refined their plans by reflecting on their notebook entries, the progress they were making toward their goals, and the efficacy of the approaches they were using.

The results suggest that teachers can use SRL strategies to improve students' academic work even while adhering to a prescribed standardized curriculum within an urban setting. Teaching students how to use self-regulation strategies yielded significantly higher rates of homework completion, better performance on a content examination, and self-reported improvement in their approaches to learning. This six-week intervention appeared to be especially effective for students in the lower-performing SRL class. The results also suggest that teachers interested in helping their students learn how to use SRL strategies effectively could adapt a three-phase approach by conducting mini-lessons and classroom discussions on ways students could use specific SRL strategies to enhance their learning, encouraging students to chart their progress in using these strategies, and helping students engage in reflective thought on how they could improve their use of SRL strategies.[9] The results also indicate that teachers might revise formative assessments to include multiple options for students to self-assess their own work (e.g., develop their own rubrics to self-assess their work and hand the self-assessments in with their completed assignments) and then use these self-assessments as a focal point in student-teacher conferences on how students can use SRL strategies to become better learners.

When transferring into classroom practice the research on students' use of SRL strategies, teachers often face strong headwinds. Hamman, Berthelot, Saia, and Crowley monitored teachers' classroom instruction and found that they devoted about 7 percent of their classroom time to coaching students to use SRL strategies and more time to such activities as quizzing (17 percent), interacting with students (29 percent), and providing direct instruction on items in the curriculum (47 percent).[10] In order to deflect these headwinds, educators may benefit from an approach that uses a slightly different language.

Because terms related to self-regulated learning can be confusing—or even off-putting to some educators, another term, *good learners*, may be more useful. Teachers, administrators, students, and parents often resonate positively to discussions that focus on helping students become good learners—individuals who advanced their learning by taking initiative, exercising curiosity, self-planning, self-monitoring, and self-evaluating their efforts.

THE CASE FOR FOCUSING ON GOOD LEARNERS

To gain a better look at how students viewed being a good learner and which activities they engaged in when they are good learners, I asked them. Their answers are important. Because individuals tend to self-regulate to a task as they understand the nature of the task,[11] students' own view of being a good learner provides valuable information on how they self-regulate as learners.

For the past four years, I've been collecting students' descriptions of their learning using two prompts: (1) "Think about a time in class when you felt you were being a 'good learner' and describe the situation," then (2) "Describe the two to three specific things that you did in this situation that made you a 'good learner.'"

Following the research of Deci and Ryan,[12] I used a five-point scale to score students' responses. Each point on the scale—referred to as a level—reflects a different stance toward learning. In descriptions scored at the lower end of the scale, students characterized good learning as paying attention and following a teacher's lead. Their responses suggested that, for them, learning was a spectator sport. Good learners simply followed their teachers' leads. One student described being a good learner in this way: "I just pay attention to what's happening. There's really nothing to be a good learner. You just have to pay attention."

Descriptions scored in the middle of the scale reflect students' use of basic study skills. In these responses, students indicated that being a good learner involved studying hard and committing their lessons to memory. A student at this level described being a good learner in these terms: "I wrote down important details about the lesson. Then later I used the notes to study for the quiz."

At the higher end of the scale, students' descriptions reflect a clear understanding that they were agents of their own learning. Good learners, in this view, thought about what they knew or did not know, developed plans accordingly, monitored these plans as they unfolded, and evaluated the outcome. A student at this level provided this example: "We were correcting answers to a topic that was hard for me to understand. . . . I engaged my teacher in a discussion about the rules of math surrounding that subject. . . . I got a red pen out and wrote the steps for each problem I got wrong to compare with my original steps."

In one high-performing district, for example, I asked about three hundred students from kindergarten through eighth grade their perspectives on being a good learner. Students in grades 2 through 8 wrote their own responses to the survey questions. Teachers in grades K through 1 met individually with students, asked the questions, and recorded students' responses verbatim.

Across all grade levels, as outlined in figure 9.1, students' responses clustered between level 2 (work hard, follow directions) and level 3 (take good notes, study hard for a test; $M = 2.47$). These results were consistent with those from two similar suburban districts, where the students' responses also centered just below the midpoint of the scale. Most of the students (78 percent) responded as good students at level 1, level 2, or level 3. Fewer students (22 percent) responded as good learners at level 4 or level 5.

Overall, about one-third of the cases (36 percent) indicated that they were a good learner when they engaged in level 1 activities, such as not fooling around and listening attentively to their teacher. A number of students (19 percent) described being a good learner in terms of level 2 activities, such as working hard at their assignments and handing their work in on time. Almost a quarter of the students (23 percent) said they were good students when they engaged in level 3 actions, such as studying hard, reviewing their notes, and checking their work before they handed it in. In fewer instances (14 percent), students used level 4 descriptions that they were good learners when they took the initiative to address issues that confused them (e.g., ask questions, go to extra help sessions). Relatively few students (8 percent) used level 5 terms to describe being a good learner as self-reflecting on their own work ("I realized I did not know this and decided to stop fooling myself"), developing a plan, and monitoring the effectiveness of the plan.

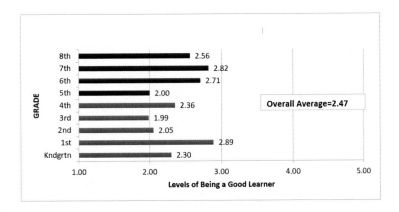

Figure 9.1. Results of good learner survey by grade (*n* = 294).

When asked to describe situations where they felt that they were good learners, most students identified occasions when they were listening to a teacher in a classroom (31 percent), were working on an assigned activity (e.g., in-class math problem, homework, in-class worksheet; 31 percent), were taking a test and receiving a good grade (19 percent), or were working in a group on an assigned task (13 percent).

Students' responses may be rooted in their perceptions of the classroom as a teacher-centered environment. From this perspective—one where teachers control all activities—learning is a passive activity. As stated by one student, "My role is to come to class, not misbehave, pay attention, complete assignments as directed."

MOVING FROM GOOD STUDENTS TO GOOD LEARNERS

Troubled by the consistent pattern of results I received during a four-year period from more than two thousand students in three separate school districts, I explored ways to help students move from being good students to being good learners. Working with fifth-grade teachers in a suburban, high-performing middle school, I set up a comparison between matched fifth-grade classes. In one class, the teacher focused on helping students take control of their own learning. She helped students move along the good student–good learner continuum; helped them develop skills in thinking systemically; set up broad-based questions for them to explore (e.g., "Why was the American Revolution successful?"); and helped them self-plan, self-monitor, and self-evaluate their progress in addressing the question. During classroom sessions, students worked individually using laptops, met in groups, or discussed ideas with partners as they constructed a systems map of the factors—and interactions among the factors—that addressed an essential question (e.g., "From 1492 to 1783, which main themes contributed to the eventual establishment of the independent United States?").

Because there was no right answer to the question, there were no tests nor quizzes. Assessments focused on students' progress in constructing systems maps that depicted the interplay among the factors that influenced the outcome of the American Revolution.

During each class session, students self-monitored their work. On a weekly basis, students self-evaluated their progress and, using this evaluation, devised plans for their next round of work. As their teacher reviewed students' self-monitoring and self-evaluation worksheets, she provided feedback to assist them in advancing their learning efforts. This student-generated information provided her with more robust feedback on students' learning than she could have gathered from a test or quiz.

The comparison class proceeded in a more traditional format. The essential question for each unit had a specific content focus (e.g., "What were the key events involved in the American Revolution?"). The teacher conducted daily lessons that focused on a specific teacher-determined objective posted at the front of the room. During each unit, the teacher gave quizzes and tests to assess students' progress.

Students in both classes completed a "Good Learner Survey" twice, once in November and again in June. As outlined in figure 9.2, in November, students in both groups had almost identical viewpoints on being a good learner: work hard, do my best, follow directions, complete assignments, do my homework, take notes, study for tests. By June, however, there was a huge difference between the two groups. In the June survey, in contrast to students in the comparison group, students in the treatment group—a group who learned how to use self-regulated learning strategies to complete problem-based assignments—indicated that they advanced their use of "good learner" practices to a much greater extent.

From a statistical viewpoint, the difference between the comparison group ($M = 2.96$) and intervention group ($M = 3.74$) is significant at the $p < 0.000$ level. When calculated as an effect size, the difference equates to a

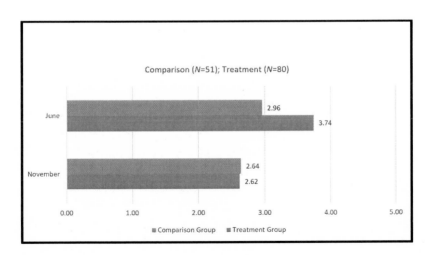

Figure 9.2. Good learner survey: Means by group.

1.02 standard deviation difference. In his review of more than eight hundred meta-analyses of educational studies, John Hattie found that the average effect size was about a 0.40 standard deviation difference between treatment and comparisons groups. [13] From this perspective, the differences between the two groups involved in this study was about 150 percent larger than typically achieved in most educational research.

When viewed in terms of the individual student progress, 55 percent of the students in the treatment group advanced by one or more levels on the good learner scale. In addition, about 20 percent of the students in the treatment group advanced by two or more units on the scale. In contrast, only 10 percent of the students in the comparison group advanced by at least one level on the scale. A scant 1 percent of the students in the comparison group advanced by two or more levels.

Students' descriptions of situations when they were good learners clustered into three categories: *classroom activities* (e.g., answering a teacher's questions correctly); *long-term projects* (e.g., working for two to three months to develop a systems map that answered a broad-based essential question); and *getting a good grade* (e.g., "I was a good learner when I got an A on my math test").

The two groups differed markedly on the occasions when they were good learners. In the intervention group, most students (65 percent) reported feeling that they were good learners as they completed long-term, investigative projects. For this group, learning involved self-planning what they wanted to learn and self-assessing their progress toward the goals they set.

In contrast to the treatment group, most of students (68 percent) in the comparison group reported that they felt like a good learner when they received a good grade ("I was a good learner when I got an A+ on my test"). This result shows the strong impact an emphasis on testing can have on students' view of learning. For this group, learning was anchored in an external evaluation: "I was a good learner when my teacher gave me a good grade."

Why are these results important? Individuals will self-regulate to a task according to their understanding of the task. If they believe that being a good learner involves paying attention and following directions—and waiting for teachers to appraise their learning efforts—then they will self-regulate accordingly. In contrast, if they believe that learning involves taking initiative, self-planning, and self-monitoring their learning efforts, then they will self-regulate accordingly.

WHAT TEACHERS CAN DO

The teachers who have successfully advanced students' skills in using self-regulated learning strategies used combinations of the following strategies:

1. Help students understand how to use SRL strategies to move from being good students to being good learners.
2. Help students plan, monitor, and evaluate their learning.
3. Help students learn how to think systemically.
4. Help students focus on broad-based essential questions.
5. Help students learn how to develop systems maps.

Good Students versus Good Learners

At the start of the year, teachers used a graphic (figure 9.3) to outline for students the differences between good students and good learners. These teachers provided specific descriptions and examples of each level of the good student–good learner continuum.

They explained that a good student at level 1 pays attention, listens to the teacher, doesn't fool around, and focuses on the task at hand and not on distractions provided by friends. Oftentimes teachers gave examples of how

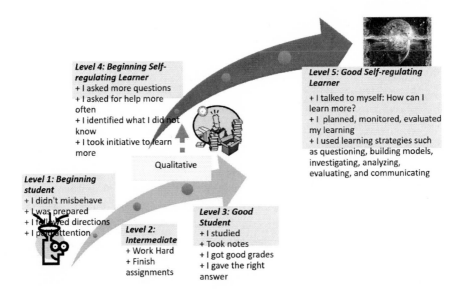

Figure 9.3.   Good student versus good learner.

students described learning at level 1: "I just pay attention to what's happening. There's really nothing to be a good learner. You just have to pay attention."

At level 2, teachers explained that good students work hard, follow directions, and work to do their best. Again, they gave examples of how students described learning at level 2: "I was listening and doing my best. I tried and did not give up easily."

Teachers described level 3 as characterized by students who take good notes in class, complete homework assignments on time, study for quizzes and tests, and aspire to get good grades. They used such examples as "I wrote down important details about the lesson. Then later I used the notes to study for the quiz."

For good students at levels 1 through 3, teachers explained that students see them, their teachers, as the epicenter for learning. As long as students follow the requirements and standards they set, all is well.

Teachers explained that a qualitative shift occurs when students transition from being good students to being good learners. They indicated that, to get to this level, students have to "jump the hedge." At level 4, they explained, students take initiative for their own learning. Often, they look for more resources or ask for help on specific items. For example, they explained, students at level 4 described how they took the initiative to learn more: "I tried the problems and asked questions to make sure I was doing the work correctly."

In concluding the discussion, teachers indicated that when students move to level 5, they reflect on what they know, figure out what they don't know, and devise strategies to learn more: "By searching harder for a good definition, I understood the term better. I normally don't go above and beyond like this, so it was a big deal for me."

Students then used the graphic to guide their own discussions. They worked in small groups to identify specific examples of how good students and good learners differed. Following the discussion, teachers handed students a good student–good learner journal (see figure 9.4). On that first day, they asked them to write one specific way they would work during the next week on becoming a better learner. At the end of the week, they asked them to review their initial entry, evaluate their progress, and identify a specific item they would work on during the next week to become a better learner. Students repeated this self-evaluation and self-planning process each week throughout the year.

During class sessions each day, teachers highlighted good student versus good learner topics as they arose and used the topics as opportunities to help students advance as good learners. The following is an example of a teacher-student interaction:

Student: How many paragraphs do I have to write for this assignment?

Teacher: That sounds like a good student question. Everyone, talk briefly with your partners. How would a good learner reframe that question? [A brief class discussion follows.]

Broad-Based Essential Question

For students to become good learners, teachers understood that they had to provide opportunities to do so. The curriculum they had used in past years reinforced a good student ethic. In the old curriculum, they provided the impetus for what students learned, set the pace for their learning, set the standards for their learning, and used those standards to evaluate their performance.

Because the essential questions they framed for each unit were often content-based, they provided a cornerstone for this good-student process. For example, in past years, one teacher used an essential question for the unit on

Week #1	After reviewing my self-assessment (above), for the first week, here's the strategy I'm going to focus on to become a better learner. (Select one strategy from the list: Questioning, Building conceptual models, Investigating, Analyzing, Evaluating, Communicating)
	This strategy will help me because….
	Here are specific actions I will use to deeply practice this strategy so I get better at using it….
	When (or if) I start to drag or lose interest, here's how I will self-ignite my efforts….
	At the end of the week this is how I'll know I succeeded….

Figure 9.4.   Self-reflection journal.

the American Revolution that was something like "What are the key events that occurred during the American Revolution?" If students used this question to guide their learning, then they would focus on learning the events, learning the names of the key actors, learning the names of key military battles, and learning the time line of the activities. Once they learned this content, they prepared themselves to restate the information on quizzes and tests—and wait for the teacher to evaluate their performance. The process was self-reinforcing for both students and their teachers. Good grades reinforced students' commitment to being good students. Good grades also confirmed to the teachers that they were doing a good job—students were learning what they were supposed to learn.

Teachers understood that they had to change the format of their instruction in order to change the self-reinforcing good-student cycle. A first step involved changing the nature of the essential questions. By changing the essential question from a content-based format that could be evaluated using objective tests (e.g., tests that used multiple-choice questions where the answers could be marked right or wrong) to one that focused on broad-based questions that prompted students to think systemically, teachers realized that they could disrupt the good-student cycle and nudge students into a good-learner cycle. For example, one teacher changed the essential question for the American Revolution to read "From 1492 to 1783, which enduring themes (relationships and interactions among key factors) contributed to the successful establishment of an independent United States of America?"

There was no one right answer to this question. She provided students with a wide assortment of web-based and print-based resources that they could use to formulate an answer. Students had free rein to set the order and path for their explorations. Instead of being the center point determining the course of students' learning, she served as a resource who helped guide them through the process.

Systemic Thinking

To introduce the idea of systemic thinking—a skill that would assist their explorations of the newly designed essential questions—the teachers used activities from students' own lives. One teacher asked students to think of four to five options they had for spending their time during the upcoming weekend. They wrote each option on a note card and placed them on their desks. In turn, she asked them to write down factors that were positive (e.g., all my friends will be there) or negative (e.g., it costs a lot of money) about each option.

To illustrate how factors interacted in a system of relationships—and how this interaction would work in their decision-making process—teachers asked students to develop systems maps. The teacher in this example asked her students to draw an illustration on a blank piece of paper showing the four options they identified for the weekend and how the interrelationships among the positive and negative factors they identified might influence their final decision.

After teachers introduced students to systems maps, they next explained how levels of influence (strength of the interactions in the map) might influence their decisions. In the previous example, the teacher asked them to revisit their maps and use a 0–3 scale to "code" the levels of influence involved in the relationships between the factors on their maps and how these levels of influence contributed to their final decisions on their weekend activities:

Level 3: **Direct cause and effect.** Teachers explained that, because so many contingencies are involved in a decision, in most cases, there might not be a single cause–effect relationship on their illustration.

Level 2: **Strong influence.** Teachers gave examples like this: If every student had a free pass to a movie they wanted to see—and the pass expired on the following Monday—then the interaction between their desire to see the movie, the free pass, and the expiration date would have a strong influence on their decision to see the movie.

Level 1: **Weak relationship.** One teacher pointed to four girls seated before her who were on the same soccer team. She said,

> Say you decided that you wanted to win your soccer game on Saturday. One factor you identified as a path to victory was making sure everyone wore their hair in a ponytail. If you did win on Saturday, your hairdo could be listed as having a weak relationship with the victory. Because the common hairdo may have helped enhance the sense of being a team and the sense of being a team could have contributed to strong team play, the hairdo could be listed as having a weak relationship with the victory.

Level 0: **No relationship.** One teacher pointed to students one by one who were ardent Boston Red Sox fans. She said, "If you decided that the best way to help the Boston Red Sox win their next game was for everyone to wear a Red Sox hat all day Saturday, whether the Red Sox won or not, then the hat-wearing factor would have no relationship at all with the outcome of the game."

During class sessions each day, as students researched topics related to the essential question they were exploring, teachers asked students to write factors and ideas on note cards, sort the note cards into piles by main ideas, transfer the factors and their evident relationships onto an illustration of how the interactions formed a system, and code the levels of influence among the relationships in the system.

Systems Maps

To help students explore the essential question, teachers provided an array of web-based and print-based materials for them to use as resources in their investigations. As explained in the prior section, students wrote on note cards the information they gathered from multiple sources and used the note cards to construct a systems map. Using a web-based software program, Lucid Charts, students constructed maps to illustrate how a multiple set of factors interacted to form a system of relationships that influenced the issue described by the essential question.

Figure 9.5 provides an example of a systems map. In answering the essential question, "From 1492 to 1783, which enduring themes (relationships and interactions among key factors) contributed to the successful establishment of an independent United States of America?" one student used a systems map to show how a set of common themes spurred on the explorers: government, wealth, determination, help from other people, and freedom of rights.

As they explored the essential question, students self-planned and self-evaluated their efforts in the process of constructing their own unique understanding of the issues involved. They used a systems map to illustrate how a complex set factors, iterative relationships between the factors, and levels of influence associated with each factor helped them explain the issue at hand in the essential question.

As would be expected from a group of learners with a wide range of individual experiences, beliefs, and perspectives, each systems map was different. There was no right or wrong answer as might be the case in a more traditional test-oriented classroom.

As students developed their systems maps, teachers worked with them to codevelop rubrics to guide their work. For example, one teacher developed a five-component rubric, with each component having four levels—excellent,

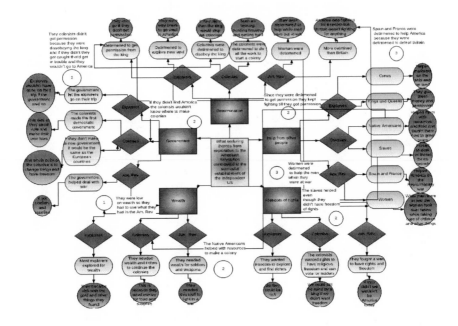

Figure 9.5. Example of a student systems map.

good, basic, and unsatisfactory. The descriptions that follow are for the excellent level:

Organization: Map is clear, well organized, and easy to understand. The
essential question is also stated accurately in the center of the map.

Main ideas: The first level (ring) of the map includes a set of main ideas
that relate to (summarize) the evidence and elaborations in the outer
rings. These main ideas are diverse (represent many aspects of the
topic) and provide a complex answer to the essential question.

Evidence (research or facts): The second level (ring) of the map includes four or more pieces of specific evidence that support each one
of the main ideas. Evidence is *not reused* in multiple areas of the map.

Relationships: At least eight links exist in the map, and a majority of the
labels on the links explain either a *direct cause and effect* or a *strong
influence* between two different *factors or main ideas*. Refer to the
relationship scale "levels of relationships within a system."

Grammar: Map follows the rules of grammar all the time.

Before students handed in their maps, they used the rubric to self-assess their
work. When students handed in completed assignments, their teachers (with-

out knowledge of students' self-evaluation scores) also assessed the maps. A comparison of teachers' versus students' ratings indicated that, overall, there was no statistical difference between the two sets of ratings. This result indicated that students and their teachers were aligned in terms of their respective understanding of the standards required for the assignment.

Before they handed in the assignment, students also completed a self-assessment of how well they self-regulated their learning (see figure 9.6). Students rated their self-regulation as excellent if they:

- Always "self-ignited" their learning,
- Always self-reflected (stepped outside of themselves to think about their learning and behavior),
- Always self-corrected (independently changed goals and behaviors to improve learning), and
- Always used strategies identified in their self-regulation journals.

The coassessment process provided information for rich student-teacher conversations. The discussion could move easily over items of common agreement to focus more on items where the ratings were discrepant. In cases where students misunderstood an item on the rubric, discussions with their

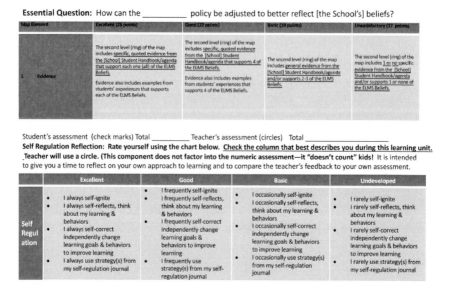

Figure 9.6.   Student self-assessment rubric.

teachers helped them clarify their understanding and, most importantly, position them to self-regulate their future learning efforts.

SUMMARY

When teachers free up instructional time by reducing the emphasis on testing, one option for using the extra time is to focus on helping students improve their use of SRL strategies to enhance their own learning. As evident in the comparison study detailed in this chapter, helping students use self-regulated learning strategies to investigate broad-based questions can have a significant relationship with students' advancing from being good students to being good learners.

NOTES

1. Boekaerts, Monique, and Lyn Corno. "Self-regulation in the classroom: A perspective on assessment and intervention." *Applied Psychology: An International Review* 54, no. 2 (2005): 199–231.

2. Zimmerman, Barry J. "Development and adaptation of expertise: The role of self-regulatory processes and beliefs." In *The Cambridge handbook of expertise and expert performance*, edited by K. Anders Ericsson, Neil Charness, Robert R. Hoffman, and Paul J. Feltovich. New York: Cambridge University Press, 2009, pp. 705–22.

3. Dignath, Charlotte, Gerhard Buettner, and Hans-Peter Langfeldt. "How can primary school students learn self-regulated learning strategies most effectively? A meta-analysis on self-regulation training programmes." *Educational Research Review* 3, no. 2 (2008): 101–29.

4. Hattie, John A. C. *Visible learning: A synthesis of over 800 meta-analyses relating to achievement.* New York: Routledge, 2009.

5. Nagle, Corey E., Barry G. Sheckley, and George J. Allen. "Enhancing urban students' use of self-regulated learning (SRL) strategies in eighth grade science classes." *Curriculum and Teaching Dialogue* 18, nos. 1–2 (2016): 27–39.

6. Zimmerman, Barry J. and Anastasia Kitsantas. "Acquiring writing revision skill: Shifting from process to outcome self-regulatory goals." *Journal of Educational Psychology* 91, no. 2 (June 1999): 241–50. Cleary, Timothy J., Barry J. Zimmerman, and Tedd Keating. "Training physical education students to self-regulate during basketball free throw practice." *Research Quarterly for Exercise and Sport* 77, no. 2 (2006): 251–62.

7. Dignath, Buettner, and Langfeldt, "Primary school students."

8. Zimmerman, "Development and adaptation." Kluger, Avraham N. and Angelo DeNisi. "The effects of feedback interventions on performance: A historical review, a meta-analysis, and a preliminary feedback intervention theory." *Psychological Bulletin* 119, no. 2 (March 1996): 254–84.

9. Cleary, Zimmerman, and Keating, "Training physical education students."

10. Hamman, Douglas, Joelle Berthelot, Jodi Saia, and Ellen Crowley. "Teachers' coaching of learning and its relation to students' strategic learning." *Journal of Educational Psychology* 92, no. 2 (June 2000): 342–48.

11. Zimmerman, Barry J. "Self-regulated learning and academic achievement: An overview." *Educational Psychologist* 25, no. 1 (1990): 3–17.

12. Deci, Edward L., and Richard M. Ryan. "The 'what' and 'why' of goal pursuits: Human needs and the self-determination of behavior." *Psychological Inquiry* 11, no. 4 (2000): 227–68.

13. Hattie, *Visible learning*.

Chapter Ten

Epilogue

A Retrospective

My view on the use of data-driven decision making (DDDM) has dramatically changed over the years. I have been a strong proponent for this work but frustrated at the lack of progress the field has made at what is truly important in public education. George Goens and I wrote *Straitjacket: How Overregulation Stifles Creativity and Innovation in Education* in 2013. Considered controversial at that time, most of the policies we wrote about just a few years ago have come to pass. We identified all that went wrong with public policy over the past twenty years or so that poisoned any reasonable attempt at making DDDM work well.

About a year ago, I spoke to a group of public school administrators from a high-performing suburban district and was surprised to find how little they knew about testing and measurement, let alone how to decide which tests to use and which to jettison. That experience, coupled with my decades of work directly in districts as a superintendent and at the university level teaching courses on this topic, led me to conclude that it was time for a change of course.

To be clear, I am not a proponent of the antitesting movement as discussed in chapter 2 on the opt-out movement. But I am concerned about over-testing, especially for those tests that teachers make little use of because of their complexity. I have concluded that most teachers and principals (and yes, central office administrators, too) know far too little measurement science to make best use of these tests and their reports. If they do use them properly, fine, but my experience tells me that most do not, which wastes money and, more importantly, precious instructional time.

My last major assignment was as superintendent in a so-called fringe urban district in Connecticut. It was designated fringe urban by the feds due to its overall demographics, but the impact of poverty on child readiness was abundantly clear. My predecessors (both outstanding superintendents) did all that they could to add instructional time to the day and year, albeit with marginal success. I tried, too, also with marginal success. The changes we collectively made over what amounted to about fifteen years of leadership were minimal in the overall scheme of things. The district was at the 24 percent poverty level when I started there in 2007 and was almost 50 percent poverty when I left in 2012. I learned a lot about what poverty truly means in the life experience of children.

What these kids need is simple: They need more instructional time. Yet, from the research on this issue (see chapter 6), it's difficult to make a substantive change, as my colleagues and I found out firsthand. When I was often asked at conferences and statewide committee meetings what our kids needed most, my response was simple and clear: *more time*. More time to catch up in kindergarten and grades 1 to 3, and then more time to stay caught up in later grades.

More time for instruction makes a big difference. Connecticut awarded my district (and others) additional resources to help improve achievement (a.k.a., test scores) during the heart of the NCLB era. We used the money to extend the school day wherever we could. Achievement rose steadily until we were doing well enough for the state to eliminate that extra funding based on the specious notion that we had changed our practices enough to sustain the changes. Well yes, we changed practices by adding time mostly (and we did other things, too, to improve instruction), but the city was unable to fill in when the extra state money was withdrawn. This same pattern was happening across Connecticut's poor cities and towns and across the nation. What happened after the extra funding was pulled? This is not rocket science: Achievement began to decline.

For all the reasons that are covered in this book, our hopes for the benefits that a major focus on data-driven decision making might make to improve education were largely lost. As George Goens and I discussed a few years ago, DDDM has been co-opted by zealots (and entrepreneurs and corporations looking to capitalize)—those who thought turning schooling into a metric-driven industry would work.

Further, national educational policy has largely failed, as I describe in chapter 1 of this book. Little is going to change now with the recent passage of ESSA. Testing is here to stay. What we have now is a condition where educators are deluged with too much testing and too much information that they are unable to use effectively. Moreover, their schools and professional accountability programs are generally focused on test data that are often utilized for the purposes beyond which they were designed. That's not a good thing for our schools and kids.

Finally, many educators still do not understand testing and measurement well enough to make good use of all this information. It's too complex a topic, and they do not have the preparation and training. Fifteen-plus years of professional development, data teams, data systems, and coursework sadly have not worked. We need to strike a better balance, letting go of some of this unnecessary testing in favor of gaining much-needed instructional time, especially in urban schools.

LESSONS LEARNED

What advice can I give? How would I proceed if reentering the superintendency or teaching graduate courses again? What should our focus be on, and how can we achieve more success? The following is a modified approach focusing on what I believe is truly important.

Find More Instructional Time by Any Means Possible — That Are Legal and Ethical!

The key to success is finding more time and using it effectively (a subject covered in chapter 9 and discussed in more depth a bit later in this chapter). Without a doubt, helping teachers improve their daily practice is useful; this is not a zero-sum proposition. That is, one strategy is not better than another, but it all adds up to improvement if properly implemented. Teachers in all schools could use more time in the classroom to teach. And poor kids who start school so far behind need more support, which almost always translates to needing more time in school and in class.

Focus on People First, Organizational Systems Second, and Testing/DDDM Third.

We are a people business. Since NCLB, we've focused on testing/DDDM first, organizational systems second, and people last, if at all, it seems. By focusing on people first, I mean to establish a culture in schools that honors teachers for their expertise. It protects them to the greatest extent possible against unfair judgments and criticism based on accountability systems that are ineffective and dangerous. It means treating kids as children and older high school kids as people, not numbers and statistics. Schools are not about tests, numbers, metrics, and comparisons. They are about kids and their emotional, social, and cognitive development. Finally, for superintendents, if you want this to change, we need to respect the principalship by "widening the corridor" of their decision making. We need to provide them cover from unfair judgments about schools failing based on misguided use of test scores.

It's All about the Culture!

(Several presidential campaigns ago, the tagline for the Democratic nominee was "It's about the economy stupid."—Bill Clinton) We have suffered under the umbrella of the NCLB accountability-driven culture for almost two decades now, and almost no one can point to success. Sure, there have been some improvements in high school graduation rates, but most test scores, including SAT and ACT, are flat. Talk to parents, and most of them want a shift away from an overreliance on testing to a renewed focus on teaching and learning. There is no better proof of this than the opt-out movement (chapter 2). Dick Ayers points out in chapter 8 a way forward, a place to start, to rebalance our approach to school and district leadership.

Which Organizational System Works?

I'm partial to the elegance of the Harvard Public Education Leadership Project (PELP) framework for school district organizational improvement.[1] There are others, and nothing here is intended to diminish their quality. The value in PELP, in my view, is a focus on what is referred to as the instructional core and organizational coherence. All district systems are viewed as supportive of that core mission, not to be developed as a means unto themselves. A key construct here is coherence—that all systems work together to support the core mission, which is effective instruction and improved learning. The instructional core is defined as the interaction among the teacher, the curriculum, and the student. This is not a quick fix for a district whose organizational structure needs serious revision. Even healthy districts will find this framework a challenge. But it is worth the effort.

Data-Driven Decision Making in Isolation Is Dangerous.

As a singular strategy, it is a misguided, misinformed approach to school improvement, usurping a great deal of time and resources to no useful end when done in isolation of a larger context. Folks will say it is part of a larger systemic approach to school improvement, but at the teacher level, they don't see it that way. And on close inspection, in too many places, I would agree with those teachers. One hears educators saying something like "I love data!" Why not say "I love tests" or "I love white boards and technology" or "I love the block schedule"? My point is that these are simply tools toward a greater goal—not ends in and of themselves. As tools, they can be useful *if properly implemented* and in a larger context; otherwise, they are a waste of time at the least and dangerous at the max, as we have seen over the past decade, with school accountability programs run amok.

On Data Teams.

Data teams are considered part and parcel of the DDDM movement, but they are treated separately here due to their pervasiveness in schools. We don't hear people say they "love data teams"; in fact, more often, teachers are loath to go to yet another meeting. Teachers often push a lot of paper during these meetings covering test data that are often too old to do anything meaningful with at the current time. Retrospectively, that might be fine but, even then, not often. In their rightful place among the broad set of tools educators use to examine relevant achievement information, the data team process can be useful. Throughout this book, I suggest that teams of teachers get together by grade or discipline to examine ways to reduce nonmandated testing. This would be a good issue for data teams to take up in their meetings.

Should You Purchase or Implement a Data Warehousing and Dashboarding System?

Probably yes but with some caveats. This all boils down to the extent to which educators understand the uses and limits of comparative statistics. New tools are making the display of data easier to view and understand, and their costs are coming down. However, implementing a system that just puts all the data within reach via easy access contributes to the problem of data information overload. If you want an example of this, check out one of the financial websites, such as www.Bloomberg.com, and try to quickly parse through and understand (1) what is going on and (2) which actions to take. Unless you are very knowledgeable about all the underlying issues, trends, and predictive algorithms, it's not going to make much sense. This is akin to what happens when most teachers and principals open the reams of test reports—even if on their computer screens.

The key to using these data is how they are compared. Typically, this is done as averages or percentiles that have very different uses and interpretations from one another. This is not a statistics book, so I won't go into detail here, but suffice it to say that meaningful and *properly constructed comparisons* presented in color-coded graphics can be very useful—if timely. Also, schools should make much greater use of effect size statistics for comparison purposes where possible.

On Making Change.

Superintendents and principals: Change is difficult, but don't let the perfect get in the way of the good. Commit yourself to improving the lives of your students by reducing the amount of unnecessary testing in their lives. Doing so will provide teachers more time to attend to their cognitive, social, and emotional needs. Whether you save one day or ten; whether the process is easy or hard and messy; whether you affect one school or all, one class or all, or just a few students or all does not matter. What matters most is that you start the process of broadening the operational definition of *accountability* by shifting as much paper-and-pencil summative testing as possible to authentic forms of assessment. Commit to putting in place the seeds of change that will truly make a difference in your school or classroom.

On Accountability Programs.

Accountability is more than testing. Too many of the tests in use today are summative in nature, mostly the result of twenty years of misguided policies imposed on schools. There are many formative tests that can be much more useful but often are not for failure to fully implement and use the results properly. Any nonmandated test used improperly or not fully is a waste of time and money. I'm going to repeat that point: If you don't fully and properly use a test, then you are wasting time and money. Either train teachers to comprehensively and consistently use these, or drop them. Teachers too often feel a need to over-test to justify grades. Provide better training and support for faculty to use more authentic assessments.

On Assessment Audits.

Most assessment audits miss a key point. If you want to know the true value of a test, then just ask teachers what they do with the results. You can skip the long, drawn-out committee report development process. Try issuing an anonymous online survey of teachers on what they think about and how they use each of the tests in your school or district. You will be surprised at the results!

For Boards of Education.

Boards play a crucial role in promoting sound practices around school culture and accountability programs and focusing energy in schools around what is important. In this case, it truly does all start at the top. Boards should minimize the minutia at their meetings and ask the administration to provide meaningful updates on key aspects of the district's strategic plan and improvement efforts. No matter how well-intentioned principals and teachers may be, if they see fighting at the top of the organization or misguided focus, then they are going to keep their heads down, follow directions, and be unwilling to experiment with new practices or ideas to keep their jobs.

MY BACKGROUND AND HOW I ARRIVED AT THESE CONCLUSIONS

You may not find the next section of great interest, but I include it here in some detail to reveal the experiences that led me to my conclusions and why I wrote this book. Feel free to skip over this section if the previous recommendations ring true to your own experiences. However, if you would like to know what brought me to this point, then I invite you to read on!

My journey began in earnest with doctoral work at the University of Connecticut in the early 1980s. After completing coursework and developing several potential draft dissertation proposals, my major advisor left the university. Fortunately, I was picked up by another professor, and that changed my professional career. Ed Iwanicki was, and is still, well known for his work in teacher evaluation, and he had strong connections to the Connecticut State Department of Education, which was interested in the just-emerging teacher competency movement. A long story made short, my dissertation was the validation study for Connecticut beginning teacher competencies.[2] Given the importance of this study to the field, it was extensive and exhaustive. The results were enacted into law and became the basis on which new teachers were initially certified in Connecticut. It also thrust me into the world of data.

There were a lot of competencies on that list: eighty-five in all in thirteen categories. They were unwieldly to operationalize, but the field pressed on. Concerned about the length and complexity of that list, the Connecticut State Department of Education convened a small working group to reconceptualize a new, shorter document. We did, and it was put into practice, only to find educators saying that it was now too short and did not provide enough detailed information about what to look for to determine competency. That was an early revelation for me that what appeared straightforward to some was not so for the field of practice.

In the years that followed, I remained interested in teacher evaluation but never found a good solution. To this day, I don't think the field has succeeded in committing to paper a set of observable skills for this purpose. There are such folks as Elliot Eisner who believe it was folly from the outset to attempt to quantify the art of teaching.[3] I had dinner with him, along with several New Hampshire school administrators around that time, and he was polite but critical of Connecticut's efforts. As a young principal, newly minted with a doctorate from UConn, I was taken aback. I now recognize the wisdom of his words so many years ago.

Since NCLB and now doubling down with ESSA, the feds are still requiring teachers to be evaluated via student test scores (albeit providing states a bit more leeway on how to proceed). As I discuss in chapter 4, this is even worse than attempting to apply a robust set of teaching competencies to the art of teaching. True, ESSA does permit states to try a different approach (largely in reaction to the testing opt-out movement), but it remains to be seen how many states remove these shackles that so constrain teaching creativity and innovation.

After earning my PhD in 1984, I became the curriculum director for Barrington, Rhode Island, a wealthy suburban school district just outside of Providence. A couple years later, they changed the title to assistant superintendent, and in 1988, I was appointed superintendent upon the retirement of my predecessor.

Although I maintained a strong interest in teacher evaluation, my position now required that I look at broad school district improvement, not just at one school. That began my efforts at dabbling with a systems approach to school improvement and, of necessity, data-driven decision making. I was interested, fascinated may be a better term, in how a systems approach to organizational development could help improve our schools. I went on to implement this approach in all my superintendencies. Systems thinking and a systems approach rely on the extensive use of data.

I called on theorists and practitioners in the business world for guidance, as precious little work was being done in education. Strategies like Peter Drucker's management by objectives[4] and Peter Senge's learning organization but more importantly his focus on systems principles for effective leadership[5] were the major drivers of my thinking. Later, Six Sigma was a new interest.[6]

My district improved, which opened opportunities for new professional positions. As I look back on it, though, I often think of the opportunities missed to focus on "people first, organization second, and DDDM third." What I remember most fondly about my Barrington years is what the athletic director said to me at his retirement ceremony: "When the financial floor fell in, Phil maintained our sports programs." Rhode Island had one of the earliest legal challenges to its school financial aid system, and when the state lost the case, Barrington lost virtually all its state aid, creating a local financial crisis. We managed through it with limited damage. During this time, my focus on systems and data waned, as one might suspect.

In 1993, I went to Avon, Connecticut, as their new superintendent, hired on my platform that applying a systems approach to school improvement was an effective methodology for improving learning and test scores. I was also interested in community-based strategic planning as an effective vehicle for identifying key goals and gaining broad-based support for those initiatives. Implementing both, test scores went up—both state-administered achievement tests and SAT scores.

Sometime around 1995 or 1996, Senator Chris Dodd (Democrat) spoke to Connecticut superintendents and urged us to take up the mantle of strong school accountability. He warned that, if we failed to do so, then the feds would do it for us. History details what happened next with the failure of Goals 2000 and the passage of No Child Left Behind the following year (see chapter 1). Thus, systems thinking and data-driven decision making were clearly now in vogue.

Just a couple years later, in 1997, my alma matter called, asking if I was interested in a professorial position to codify this emerging field of data-driven decision making. I left Avon and began my time at UConn. Tom Peters's book *The Circle of Innovation* came out a few years later, which further convinced me that we needed to apply those techniques to schools, but there was little guidance at the time as to how to proceed. [7]

I wrote two books while at UConn on this emerging field of data-driven decision making, [8] plus a bunch of papers on the topic. I also did a lot of consulting, trying to help educators do this tough work. My work tended to focus on the technology needed to empower educators to do this work. Data warehousing was a relatively new field at the time, more applicable in banking and retail than other fields and not yet applied to schools at all.

That became my focus midway through my UConn years, as I realized there was little we could do in schools if teachers and principals had to sift through reams of paper reports to find pertinent information on which to formulate improvement strategies. And the challenge of computing comparative statistics was overwhelming without all the data in one place, easily accessible electronically. Compare this to the private sector, where data systems and analytical engines were in place and improving. Schools were being left in the dust.

Working with the Connecticut Academy for Education in Science, Math, and Technology and in partnership with private industry, we developed a working data warehouse for schools. Once we had all the data in one place, I was surprised to find that was not the real problem. The major issue was that educators did not know what to do with that information. This realization led to a redesign of my major teacher responsibility and courses at UConn on DDDM—a new focus on the basic statistical knowledge needed to know what to do to properly interpret the large amount of information now at educators' fingertips in these data warehouses. This problem remains the main obstacle today.

In 2007, I wondered whether all of this "science" could be applied effectively to improve an urban district. I was hired in Bristol, Connecticut, based on my work with DDDM and success in earlier districts raising test scores. Bristol was a city at a juncture at the time. The poverty rate when I started was 24 percent. It would go one of two ways: become more successful and move toward more of a suburban district or become poorer and more of an urban inner city. I enjoyed broad support from my board of education and all the city and financial boards.

We were making early progress, when the financial bottom fell with the advent of the Great Recession of 2008. And adequate yearly progress (AYP) was demoralizing. Wealthy suburban schools like those I had served in earlier would not experience this AYP pain until much later due to the quirks of how AYP was engineered.

I often tell the story of one Bristol elementary school that had worked extremely hard all year to get off the NCLB "needs improvement list" and that the local and state papers renamed the "failing school list." We had several of our schools (but not all) on this list. When the new scores came out, this school missed the average score needed by a hair, thus was again labeled as "failing."

The principal, faculty, staff, and parents were devastated—demoralized is perhaps a better term. I could see and feel their pain. Knowing that averages don't tell the full story (statistically speaking), I asked my curriculum department to compute effect size improvement scores by longitudinal cohort for every possible cohort in this school over the past three years. In other words, I wanted to track kids from third to fourth to fifth grades, analyzing growth in their scores using a universal metric. This was a matched cohort analysis, only computing scores on kids who were in the school for at least one full year to the next or more. The idea was to prove to staff and parents that their efforts were working for kids who were in their school over a period of time.

All these calculations indicated that kids improved and improved dramatically so but not enough in the aggregate to get off the "failing list." For example, large groups of kids might have improved by 50 percent or more as they moved from third to fourth grade, but they were still below the AYP bar, so there was no publicity credit. Armed with this new set of stats and Power-Point slides, I convened the faculty, staff, and parents of this school the following week and showed them proof that their work had paid off for the clear majority of kids in this school and that they should not believe the state and federal governments, along with the press, that they had "failed." They were making great progress with these kids, changing their lives and academic trajectories. They should feel good about their work.

This was a turning point for me, when I began to seriously question the efficacy of relying so heavily on data and systems to evaluate and improve schools and school districts. I subsequently computed similar scores for all cohorts throughout the district for all our schools. In just about every case, we identified real growth, whereas the yearly AYP numbers did not improve. (For those wondering, there is a statistical reason for this that has to do with the types of metrics used to report the results—a topic beyond the scope of this book.)

We also developed streamlined PowerPoint slides depicting these cohort stats, color-coding the results (my introduction to dashboarding). Dark green was used to indicate strong growth; light green, moderate growth; yellow and red, no growth (warning) or negative results (color-coded by accepted practice regarding effect size growth levels). During presentations to the board of education, city council, and finance board, my goal was to communicate progress. Various board members would note that there was a lot of "green" up on the projection screen—a good thing.

Urban education was a new experience for me, having served in high-performing suburban districts prior. Bristol was an eye-opener on so many levels. I learned quickly that test scores were meaningless if teachers did not have kids in their classes consistently over time or even for a single year!

This led to my "180 First Days of School" presentation to the city council and finance board. Our most affected elementary school had an extremely high poverty and migration rate. To communicate the problem effectively and the need for more resources to help kids "catch up," I created a Power-Point slide called "180 First Days of School."

I asked the principal to research (that had to be done by hand at the time) how many kids entered or left his school each month. The numbers were staggering. The results indicated that a typical teacher in that school would start off with twenty-five kids in September and have only five of those same kids still in her class at the end of the year! The other twenty would have left sometime during the year (due to parents typically losing housing and having to move). This story made for a compelling case for more resources, which the city tried to give us. But it was tough economic times due to the Great Recession and its impact on the both the state and a relatively poor city.

Bristol also had schools recognized statewide for achievement and programming; it was a diverse district. We were also headed for state-mandated redistricting due to the in-district segregation created by differences in housing costs based on area. These were all challenging issues.

Test scores did go up in Bristol—Connecticut Mastery scores as well as SAT scores. But on reflection, I came to understand that the key issue was time—the need for more instructional time to help poor and disadvantaged kids catch up and stay competitive with their peers who started school with so many more opportunities and a broader and deeper language base.

One final note on the use of systems for organizational improvement: Based on my UConn work (and I maintained my teaching role after leaving the university in 2007 throughout my Bristol years to 2012), I retained focus on the importance of using a systems approach to improvement. As noted earlier in this chapter, I utilized the Harvard PELP model.[9] This approach remains effective today, and I would use it again if I reentered school leadership. PELP's focus is on the instructional core rather than one system or another. At the heart of the PELP framework is organizational coherence—how the various systems are organized and work together to support the interaction of teaching, curriculum, and the student to improve learning. A singular focus on data teams, for example, won't cut it in this framework.

Also central to the PELP model is the concept of the theory of action. A theory of action is the plan one makes to achieve a goal within the improvement framework. There are several key ideas inherent in how to develop, monitor, and achieve a theory of action that are beyond the scope of this book. Suffice it to say here that, properly implemented, there is likely no more powerful method of leading school improvement.

Had the financial bottom not fallen out in Bristol due to the Great Recession of 2008 and had the state not pulled funds when achievement scores improved (without realizing that the issue was sustainability), Bristol would have turned that corner. If I had it to do all over again in Bristol, unlike my other districts, I would basically do the same things except for three: I would focus on people first and systems second, and I would significantly cut back on the amount of nonmandated locally controlled testing to recapture instructional time so needed by kids who enter school so far behind. Finally, if pressed, I would have taken resources out of the two high schools to extend the school day for kindergartners citywide.

RELATED EXPERIENCES

Schools need a strong, valid, and reliable benchmark on which to base instructional improvement efforts. NWEA's Measure of Academic Progress (MAP) test is the best in the business. I won't go into details here; suffice it to say that I was well aware of its strengths.

Thus, I brought in NWEA MAP halfway through my time in Bristol to create a stronger benchmark for improvement, knowing that with MAP we could better track student progress and identify specific learning deficits. I had used NWEA MAP before in Avon and Barrington and felt it would complement progress on improving the organization via the PELP framework.

No doubt it would have if principals and faculty knew what to do with the results! NWEA MAP is powerful but complex. The reports are detailed, so much so that infrequent review for those not using it every day caused confusion, as they often did not remember what all the numbers and charts meant. The district abandoned NWEA MAP shorty after I left.

I was asked to join the NWEA board during my Bristol tenure and did so enthusiastically. NWEA is a nonprofit organization, and I felt then, and still do today, that its assessment products are the best available. The trick is to know what to do with them. In retrospect, I suspect that the financial crisis Bristol experienced led as much to the academic downturn as any other issue. Had the bottom not fallen out, I'm confident that we would have had the time and resources to effectively use NWEA MAP within a broader framework of organizational and instructional improvement—assuming we could add instructional time somehow.

FINAL COMMENTS

Schools are testing too much because they think it's important to do so. Some testing is needed, but much of it is unnecessary, duplicative, or goes unused or is not used properly. Data systems and data warehousing have not worked well because educators don't know how to use comparative statistics. The recent move to charting and dashboarding helps, but one needs to go deeper to make meaningful changes. Leadership should work to create a culture where teachers feel safe and secure in sharing their true feelings about all the tests used in their schools.

These issues are particularly important for urban school districts. Why urban? Because that is where the greatest challenge and need exists, and it is where we are wasting the most amount of time where it is needed the most.

What about suburban schools? There are lessons to be learned here, too. And there is crossover between urban and suburban districts with respect to systems and organizational improvement, state and federal testing and standards, and the politics of the superintendency. But the major difference between the two is the extra instructional time disadvantaged kids need in urban schools. That is my main motivation for writing this book.

Administration needs to create a culture of safety and security to promote principal and teacher experimentation with new instructional approaches.

This is especially true for any practice that might affect teacher evaluation or student grading, where parent complaints might come into play.

Most importantly, schools are not about tests, numbers, metrics, and comparisons. They are about kids and their emotional, social, and cognitive development. I wish you well in your journey to improve the lives of kids and teachers in your schools.

NOTES

1. Childress, Stacey, Richard F. Elmore, Allen Grossman, and Susan Moore Johnson. *Managing school districts for high performance: Cases in public education leadership.* Cambridge, MA: Harvard Education Press, 2007.

2. Streifer, Philip A., and Edward F. Iwanicki. "The validation of beginning teacher competencies in Connecticut." Paper presented at the Annual Meeting of the American Educational Research Association, Chicago, IL, March 31–April 4, 1985. ERIC document reproduction services no. 265 148.

3. Eisner, Elliot W. "Educational connoisseurship and criticism: Their form and functions in educational evaluation." In *Evaluation models: Viewpoints on educational and human services evaluation*, edited by George F. Madaus, Michael S. Scriven, and Daniel L. Stufflebeam. Boston: Springer Netherlands, 1983, pp. 335–47.

4. Greenwood, Ronald C. "Management by objectives: As developed by Peter Drucker, assisted by Harold Smiddy." *Academy of Management Review* 6, no. 2 (1981): 225–30.

5. Senge, Peter M. *Systems principles for leadership.* Cambridge: Massachusetts Institute of Technology, 1985.

6. Pande, Peter S., Robert P. Neuman, and Roland R. Cavanagh. *The Six Sigma way: How GE, Motorola, and other top companies are honing their performance.* New York: McGraw-Hill, 2000.

7. Peters, Tom. *The circle of innovation: You can't shrink your way to greatness.* New York: Vintage, 2010.

8. Streifer, Philip A. *Using data to make better educational decisions.* Lanham, MD: Rowman & Littlefield Education, 2002. Streifer, Philip A., with George Goens. *Tools and techniques for effective data-driven decision making.* Lanham, MD: Rowman & Littlefield Education, 2004.

9. Childress et al., *Managing school districts.*

About the Authors

Philip A. Streifer, PhD, is an author and consultant in the areas of school improvement, assessment, and testing. Phil has been a superintendent of schools, teacher, and consultant focusing on leadership development and assessment literacy. He was superintendent of Bristol (CT) Public Schools, an urban school district, as well as Avon (CT) and Barrington (RI)—both suburban, high-performing districts. Prior to assuming the Bristol superintendency, he was associate professor of educational leadership and a member of the graduate faculty at the University of Connecticut, where he taught educational leadership, evaluation, and use of data for executive decision making. He developed UConn's successful executive leadership program for superintendent certification.

Phil has written three books on educational improvement and use of data. *Using Data to Make Better Educational Decisions* (Rowman & Littlefield Education, 2002) was copublished with the American Association of School Administrators. In 2013, he cowrote a book on educational policy with George Goens titled *Straitjacket: How Overregulation Stifles Creativity and Innovation in Education* (Rowman & Littlefield).

Phil has been a member of the Northwest Evaluation Association Board of Directors, a regent for the University of Hartford, president of the Connecticut Coalition for Justice in Education Funding, chair of the Connecticut Association of Urban Superintendents, and board member for the Educational Records Bureau in New York City.

His PhD in educational administration is from the University of Connecticut; he also holds a master's degree in school administration from Central

Connecticut State University and a bachelor's degree in music education from the Hartt School at the University of Hartford.

Barry G. Sheckley, PhD, is professor emeritus, University of Connecticut, and has devoted more than thirty years researching how individuals learn best. His research received wide recognition through many publications, and Dr. Sheckley has received several national awards for research excellence, a lifetime achievement award for outstanding contributions, and an honorary medal from the University of Connecticut.

Richard Ayers, EdD, is a retired school administrator with more than thirty-five years of experience, initially as a high school principal and more recently as a district superintendent of schools. Many of his insights on the transforming culture of schools are related to his graduate-level teaching of philosophy and ethics in education, as well as educational leadership. He is retired and lives in central New Hampshire.